RESURRECTED

Faith

the heart of a
CONTENDER

D. Greg Ebie

Perfect for your small group!

Don't miss out! Be sure to order your copy of the
Resurrected Faith: The Heart of a Contender
companion study guide.

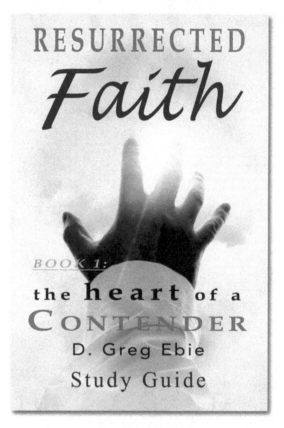

Visit **www.firmfoundationtoday.com/books**
or your favorite bookseller.

Get a free copy of the study guide and more when you enroll in our
online course or register for a webinar at:

https://FirmFoundationToday.com/ResFaithOnline

Plus save 50% with the coupon code "R-F-BookSeries"

What others are saying...

D. Greg Ebie provides from Scripture and his own experience the tension to know the faith established at Creation and the fulfillment of it through the person of Jesus. His heart's desire is for each of us to contend earnestly with a living faith. *Resurrected Faith* delivers a passion to know Jesus, the author of our faith, with scriptural principles and personal illustrations.

Doug Clay
General Superintendent of the Assemblies of God

After close to fifty years in ministry, I have read a lot of books. Today, I don't read books in search of more knowledge or facts. My desire is for the words on the page to encourage me to be more like Jesus with fresh faith that strengthens me to finish strong as I approach the end of my journey. *Resurrected Faith* does that. With the new word "faithing," Greg encourages us to allow the Holy Spirit to enable us to live what we believe. After reading each chapter, I felt alive again like I had gone back a little closer to the day when Jesus first saved me.

Dave Gross
Pastor Columbus, Ohio

Resurrected Faith will take you on a journey of self-examination and deep introspection. Throughout the book, I found even the most obvious and familiar truths were brought back to life with a new awareness and conviction of the Holy Spirit. Today believers are often more familiar with "resurrected flesh" rather than "resurrected faith." Greg is transparent with his journey on that perilous gauntlet. Most Christians want to contend for their faith but are simply not sure how to go about it. Even those who know how to contend often lack the courage to contend. Greg's insights into Jude's short letter are inspirational and reveal the necessary steps to contend for the faith without being contentious.

Mark Biel
Pastor Kinsman, Ohio

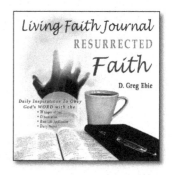

What others are saying...

When reading *Resurrected Faith*, one quickly catches the passion and urgency of Greg's heart for the condition of the Western Church in modern times. The Church stands at a crucial crossroads. Will we continue down a lethargic spiritual path and cease to be a change agent for the Kingdom of God in our culture and communities? Or will we come alive again with a burning passion for "the faith that was once and for all handed down to the saints?" This is the living faith Greg encourages us to contend for—a practical faith lived out with love to bring the needed change to all those touched by it. Read on and accept the challenges to live out in spirit and in truth what Greg identifies as "the first faith." *Resurrected Faith* ignites the life of Christ in us, which is the game-changer our world needs.

Steve Walent
Missionary, Germany

My dear brother, D. Greg Ebie issues a call of accountability for Christians and the Church to a passionate resurrected faith, which embodies an intimate relationship with Jesus Christ by the Holy Spirit. His personal illustrations and biblical exegesis illuminate the message of a living, vibrant faith. *Resurrected Faith* is a clarion call to the twenty-first century Body of Christ to live a contagious, genuine Christ-like love to transform both individual lives and a society seeking true hope.

Dr. David Bittinger
Dallas, Texas

Resurrected Faith provides the answer for a stagnate church, and was a life-changing read for me, challenging me to put away the sin that crept into my life, so I can love people as Jesus loves. If I genuinely love God and love my neighbor, I cannot be silent; I must "contend for the faith." This book will surely convict, comfort, guide, and inspire anyone who reads it.

Johnny McWilliams
Myrtle Beach, South Carolina

RESURRECTED FAITH
The Heart of a Contender

Firm Foundation Publishing
ISBN-13: 978-1-7364959-3-3

firmFOUNDATION

FUEL FOR YOUR FIRE | FUEL FOR YOUR LIFE

All communication may be sent to:

Firm Foundation Publishing
D. Greg Ebie
9815 Nichols Rd.
Windham, OH 44288
greg@firmfoundationtoday.com

Foreword

Dr. Stan Tharp

I began my journey into full-time pastoral ministry over 40 years ago as an optimistic and somewhat naïve 22-year-old youth and associate pastor. Those days of youth retreats, outreaches, and puppet show performances (Jim Henson's Muppets had just been "born") are a distant but pleasant memory.

I was grateful for a handful of dedicated adult leaders and reliable teenagers who helped me stumble my way through those years. We developed healthy discipleship for our group with practical ministry reaching opportunities outside our walls.

D. Greg Ebie was one of those reliable teens and was one of my "go-to people." His love for the LORD was evident at a young age.

He was always interested in helping reach new people with the love of Christ and was eager to help disciple the youth within our group.

I've known Greg ever since. I have stayed in touch with his pastoral career. Like me, he started as a youth pastor and then took on the role of senior pastor. We've both learned a lot through the years.

Greg gave me a copy of the original edition of *Resurrected Faith: Contending to Know Jesus the Cornerstone.* As a fellow author, I encouraged him in his plan to revise that book into the current three-volume series *Resurrected Faith.* These books with their companion study guides are rightly named by the person who wrote them.

The Heart of a Contender reveals Greg's passion, having contended for the faith his whole life. Whether sharing his faith with high school peers, or his congregation of almost 20 years, Greg is a student and proponent of God's word.

Quick to cut to the chase, Greg identifies how much of American faith is woefully lacking and reminiscent of the spiritual tragedy of the church in Sardis. In the Apostle John's Revelation, Jesus told this church, *"I know your deeds; you have a reputation of being alive, but you are dead. Wake up! Strengthen what remains"* (Rev. 3:1-2, NIV).

Jesus' warning against dead faith trying to look alive is timeless and applies now as much as it did 2,000 years ago. Greg keenly calls to the unspoken yearning of many Christians today when he says, "You hear Jesus' call and feel the need to be revived deep within your heart. You don't understand all the reasons why. You just know something is wrong…You have a longing to be alive again, a yearning for resurrected faith."

The Heart of a Contender will take you on a journey to renew your heart for God. Greg will help you listen for the cry of your own heart for a more genuine passion for God. You'll learn about *"faithing"* because faith is a word that should have been recognized as a verb a *long* time ago!

Be ready for the uphill climb to identify dead faith so prevalent today. Learn how to take a stand like saints of old, contending together for vibrant living faith.

Greg doesn't make false promises, the journey won't be easy, but then, the very word "contender" speaks of our fight for the faith. Our struggle is nothing new. The Apostle Paul spoke of our spiritual battle, saying, *"our struggle is not against flesh and blood, but against the rulers, against the authorities, against the powers of this dark world and against the spiritual forces of evil in the heavenly realms"* (Eph. 6: 12, NIV).

Rather than be engaged, contemporary Christianity relies too much on convenience. As Greg urges us, "Don't hit your spiritual snooze button and drift back into a religious slumber. Hear the alarm. An impotent, lifeless faith has infected your church and mine. None of us are immune to this sickness that hides in the darkened corners of our hearts."

Don't stop now! Resist the temptation to lay this book aside. Instead, keep reading and enjoy the journey before you. You're going to be thankful for the impact of *Resurrected Faith* in your life.

RESURRECTED FAITH

The Heart of a Contender

Resurrected Faith

By faith Abraham heard God's call to travel to a place he would one day receive as an inheritance; and he obeyed, not knowing where God's call would take him.

Hebrews 11:8 (VOICE)

Most people would think Abe was crazy. However, the LORD[1] told him to "go to the land I will show you," so he told his wife they were moving (Gen 12:1, NLT). First known as Abram until God changed his name, Abraham uprooted his household, leaving his hometown and everything familiar for an unknown destination.

Like quitting your job, selling your house, loading everything you own in a U-haul, and setting out with no forwarding address, Abraham's actions seem insane. I can hear my kids complain, "We're never going to see grandma and grandpa again." Then, barely out the driveway, they all cry, "I miss my friends already."

What Abraham did was not logical. Without a GPS location to guide his journey, Abraham obeyed God's voice, ultimately moving over six hundred miles to the land of Canaan.

Today, when believers take a step of faith to obey God, it does not make sense either. Family and friends might think you are crazy because acting in faith is considered irrational by those who have not heard God's call.

The story of Abraham's call illustrates how the Christian life is a pilgrimage, a journey of faith. We also discover how the LORD[1] leads His people.

Jesus seldom leads His followers with just head knowledge. The LORD does not lay out a reasonable plan for us to follow from start to finish. Instead, His call to walk by faith provides only enough information to take the first step. We never know where the journey of faith will take us. We only know we heard the voice of Jesus say, "Go."

The LORD will often first lead His people from a passion deep within their hearts and not rational thoughts within their heads.

We want to put our heads first with a longing to have reasons for the things we do. You and I desire a clear goal to see where we are going. We want to evaluate every step, look for any obstacle, and plan our options.

Our head does not want to venture out on a whim. Following an impulse is not safe. Reason demands we know where we are going, what it will cost, and how we will get there.

God rarely provides all the answers our rational minds desire when He communicates with us because the LORD does not start talking to our heads. Instead, Jesus begins by speaking to our hearts.

The heart responds first, leading the way as it hears Jesus' call to come and follow Him on the journey of faith.

You heard Jesus calling to you. You've listened to that still small voice and taken steps of faith to follow the path He put in your heart. That's why you are holding a book called *Resurrected Faith* in your hands. Resurrection is not logical but goes against common-sense real-world thinking as people understand it. To think what is dead can come alive again defies rational thought.

The idea of resurrected faith must sound crazy to the average person. They recognize even if faith leads us to believe in resurrection power, for one's faith to need a resurgence of life means it is dead. This kind of thinking is counterintuitive.

Still, you hear Jesus' call and feel the need to be revived deep within your heart. You don't understand all the reasons why. You just know something is wrong. You have a heartfelt desire for more. You are not satisfied with the routine of religious activity. Deep down, you know the abundant life Jesus promised is more than an emotionally moving worship service to get you through the week. You long for freedom from the pitfalls of sin, but you don't know how to start or where to turn.

You have a longing to be alive again, a yearning for resurrected faith. I, too, long for Jesus to pour out His Spirit to revive us again with living faith. *Resurrected Faith* will show us the way.

In book one, *Resurrected Faith: The Heart of a Contender,* we will be awakened to the crisis of dead faith that threatens our families and churches. While we are powerless to revive what is dead, the Holy Spirit wants to place a burning passion in our hearts to contend for the faith. These are the first steps on our journey together to receiving a resurrected faith.

With the Spirit's help, we will also take a closer look at ourselves. We will look into the mirror of God's word to expose the enemy within and understand our identity as followers of Jesus. Then, we will learn how to contend without being contentious because our struggle is not against other believers but to fight together for a living faith. Book one concludes with how to persevere with the heart of a contender.

Books two and three, *Resurrected Faith: Your Passion to Know Jesus the Cornerstone* and *Winning the Battle for Living Faith* will continue our journey. Ah, but we don't want to get ahead of ourselves because every journey begins with the first step.

I pray the Holy Spirit speaks to our hearts in the pages that follow. Avoid your desire to put your head first, but, allow God to plant His word deeply within you, giving you the heart of a contender.

Contending Together,

D. Greg Ebie—June 2021

Notes: Introduction

[1] LORD – Throughout this book, you will see LORD printed with all caps as a reminder of who Jesus is. Often our English translations of the Bible will use "LORD" in the Old Testament as a designation of the unspeakable and eternal name of God, **Yahweh** meaning the "I Am" or "the Existing one" (see Exodus. 3:14-15). The scriptures teach us, *"The LORD our God, the LORD is one"* (Deut. 6:4, emphasis mine). Today, we understand God as a trinity—three in one. God the Father, God the Son (Jesus), and God the Holy Spirit exist in an unbroken unity and are recognized as the eternal God. Jesus Christ is our Savior and LORD.

Chapter 1

A Singular Heart's Cry

*The word of God burns in my heart; it is like fire
in my bones.*

Jeremiah 20:9 (VOICE)

The sickness began in late December 2019, far away in a city few of us in America knew or recognized. Soon everyone learned of Wuhan, China, because the virus knew no boundaries. COVID-19 not only crossed international borders, but the virus also spread across every ethnic, economic, political, religious, and social class imaginable.

On March 11, 2020, less than three months after the outbreak began, the World Health Organization declared COVID-19 a global pandemic. Four days later, the U.S. Center for Disease Control advised no gatherings of fifty or more people. From that day forward, all of us felt the pandemic's impact in one way or another.

By the first anniversary of the pandemic, the number of COVID-19 confirmed cases worldwide rose to over 118 million, with more than 2.62 million deaths. The U.S. reported nearly one-fourth of the global cases at 29.2 million and one-fifth of the deaths at 529,263.[1]

These were far from impersonal numbers.

While individuals covered their faces with masks to stop the spread of the sickness, COVID-19 was not a faceless disease. You and I can see the faces and speak the names of family and friends who either had the disease or died from it. You might be one of those millions who survived the infection.

Today, we face another pandemic far more dangerous than COVID-19. However, you won't hear about it on the news. Family and friends won't talk about it or share posts on social media.

The impact of this pandemic is more significant than a tally of global cases or deaths. The shockwaves are more severe than any economic crisis, and no government bailout will help alleviate the problems caused by this deadly disease.

The consequences of this spiritual pandemic are eternal.

Dead faith ravages our families, communities, and churches. Like COVID-19, dead faith knows no boundaries. The denominational lines we draw to delineate our Christian churches are powerless to stop the spread of dead faith. In truth, these countless religious borderlines show how widespread the problem is. Jesus established one Church united in Him, and not many churches divided by man-made doctrinal boundaries.

The Holy Spirit wants to awaken us to a pandemic threatening the vitality and life-giving power of the Church.

Don't hit your spiritual snooze button and drift back into a religious slumber. Hear the alarm. An impotent, lifeless faith has infected your church and mine. None of us are immune to this sickness that hides in the darkened corners of our hearts.

Now is the time to come to Jesus, who alone can take what is dead and make it alive again through His resurrection power.

Life-defining Moments

You never know when something will happen to shape your life. Whether the event is big or small, we never know when times of change will happen. Looking back, we just know something is different now. These experiences divide time in two—before and after our transformation.

An opportunity to shape our lives is before us. I pray the Holy Spirit will bring about a faith resurrection to transform and change us from the inside out. You and I may never be the same because we met together in the pages of the *Resurrected Faith* series. Our ambition is to see what is dead come alive again—a life-defining moment with living faith awaits us.

I've experienced many of these times in my life. At the age of twelve, the Holy Spirit whispered a call to ministry, and my answer set me on a path that shaped my life.

At my ordination, I felt more than the hands of elders praying for me. I sensed the nail-scarred hands of Jesus upon my head to anoint and set me apart. God engraved His word on my heart to serve Him and His Church with faithful integrity.

In his book *The Purpose Driven Church,* Rick Warren's message brought me an unexpected insight to see ministry as a covenant-calling rather than a career-calling. Like the marriage covenant made with my wife Susie, unfailing love for Jesus's Church grew in my heart through this change of perspective.

When my dad died and his voice of godly wisdom was silenced, I was broken. But God used this time to instill a fearless faith to hear the still small voice of the Holy Spirit within me. God increased my confidence, empowering me to follow the Spirit's leading without question.

Often the LORD used my life-defining moments to encourage me in times of unexpected difficulty. Milestones like how the Spirit spoke to me as a teenager with the promise God would continue His good work in me and "bring it to completion" helped me persevere (Phil. 1:6).

Undoubtedly, you experienced your own unique and important events shaping the person you are today. Life-defining moments stand as memorials, a testimony of transformation in our lives. Like the caterpillar turning into a butterfly within its cocoon, each life-defining moment works to change us into the person we are becoming—the man or woman God always intended us to be.

My memories of these times encouraged me during life's storms. Without a doubt, God used these moments to define who I am. No turning back—I don't want to return to the me I used to be.

Little did I know at the beginning of 2017 how the LORD[2] again brought me to a crucial crossroad of change. Unexpected conflict and division the previous year tore at my heart and the hearts of the congregation where I served as pastor. I'm thankful God brought us through this time of testing with healing and a renewed hope for the future. The Holy Spirit gave me a strategy that I prepared to put into action.

I met with Pastor Mark Biel, a friend and mentor, excited to share my God-given vision. However, the Holy Spirit had other intentions for our meeting. Directed by the LORD, he made a statement that proved to be another life-defining moment.

He said, "Greg, I want to pray God will give you *a singular heart's cry.*"

From reading church history about the reformers and great revivalists, he told me how God gave many of them a particular vision and focus. He shared the example of the Moravian missionaries Johann Dober and David Nitschmann. In 1732, they were willing to sell themselves as slaves to share the gospel with enslaved African in the Caribbean islands. The two boarded a ship with a singular focus, not knowing if they would ever see their family and friends who stood alongside the dock pleading with them not to go. Dober and Nitschmann responded to their cries with unwavering passion, "May the Lamb that was slain receive the reward of His suffering!"[3]

Our meeting ended with prayer, but in the months that followed, I was in the Holy Spirit's crosshair. Again and again, my friend's request flooded my thoughts.

As a busy pastor, I contemplated whether the sermons I preached and classes I taught communicated my unique desire. I paid attention to my conversations and prayers with others listening for a repeated zeal. I kept wondering, *"What is my passion, my drive?"*

I remembered my call to the ministry and the defining moments that shaped my life. When I began my second pastoral position in 1998, my goal was to serve that church for twenty-five years. Perhaps over eighteen years later, my heart cry was a refocused zeal to finish strong with the heart of a faithful shepherd.

However, my heart was still restless, filled with more questions than answers. Was there something greater—something still unknown? Was my drive bigger than me, or had I limited myself, and in turn, restricted God's purpose for my life? Did my heart's cry resonate with the heart of Jesus?

Searching for answers, the Holy Spirit led me in an unexpected direction—to think about the short epistle of Jude. Only twenty-five verses long, I began to see the depth of meaning it held for us for today. Jude's message began to burn deep within me as I reflected on the painful schism our church experienced some eighteen months earlier. And so, in August 2017, Susie and I agreed to change course. After nineteen years of pastoral ministry at Life Church, I resigned, and we said goodbye to the people we loved.

God answered my friend's prayer with a passion burning deep within my heart.

Follow Your Heart

Many people go through their lives with no idea why they do the things they do. Each day, week, and month is much like all the ones before. People get stuck in the routine of life with little or no meaning.

A singular heart's cry moves you out of the meaningless repetition of day to day life. Rather than continue an endless routine, you have a purpose for living. A personal mission statement gives you clarity of focus and a drive to keep going when others give up and quit. With a singular heart's cry, you have faith to follow your heart even when it does not make sense.

Living faith can be ours as the LORD puts a passion to "contend for the faith" into our hearts.

The purpose of *Resurrected Faith* springs from my singular heart's cry. I share a focused determination that first resonated in Jude's words written nearly 2,000 years ago. He wrote:

> *Beloved, although I was very eager to write to you about our common salvation, I found it necessary to write appealing to you to contend for the faith that was once for all delivered to the saints. (Jude 1:3)*[4]

Living faith can be ours as the LORD puts a passion to "contend for the faith" into our hearts.

Over three years in the making, I wrote *Resurrected Faith* with you in mind. I imagined us sitting in a coffee shop to talk about how we can struggle together for the faith. Jude said Jesus entrusted "the faith" to everyone who believes, so we are all responsible for the pandemic of dead faith. Your willingness to join me in this conversation tells me you see something is wrong.

Today, the invitation to follow our hearts and "contend for the faith" is ours. We want more of Jesus in our daily lives. We ache for something better, to find meaning and purpose in our religious routines. We are desperate to experience the resurrection power of God so dead faith might live again.

Paul's message to Timothy is an encouragement I hope inspires you with confidence. He wrote, "to this end we toil and strive...." Paul challenged Timothy to contend with him in a struggle filled with difficulties and dangers.[5] Together, they joined in a fight for the faith "...because we have our hope set *on the living God*" (1 Tim. 4:10, emphasis mine). Resurrection hope is found in Jesus, who overcame the strength of the grave through the power of eternal life in Him.

Our struggle for a resurrected faith cannot happen through human energy. Our best efforts will fail us.

Instead, a resurrected faith is grounded in our confident hope in the God who lives forever. With steadfast confidence, we look to the *"living God"* who will restore life within the Church and each of us who believe.

Your Heart's Cry

Whether you know it or not, you always follow your heart. Your passions drive you forward. Unfortunately, few of us can identify the cry of our hearts because our hearts are divided. Our hearts groan for many things rather than a singular heart's cry.

Dead faith restrains us from the pursuit of a singular heart's cry. Our lives and hearts are compartmentalized. We withhold part of our heart and keep it reserved for our families while giving other pieces to education and career success. Nearby, another compartment craves wealth with the power and nice things money buys. We have a place in our heart to enjoy entertainment, and another seeks out pleasure.

8

The drive for the various compartments within our hearts may grow and decline in intensity. Sometimes we want certain things more and other things less. Unchecked, any one of them could demand satisfaction regardless of the cost to the others.

If you want to identify your singular heart's cry, the starting place is to examine your three C's—your checkbook, calendar, and cares. You will learn a lot about the different desires of your heart by evaluating how you spend your money and use your time. The thoughts that keep you awake at night will identify more compartments in your heart that long for satisfaction. Worry silences the different cries of your heart because anxiety and fear rob you of the fulfillment you long for in other areas of your life.

As Christians, we also have a God-box in our hearts. We may place this special box at the center of our hearts and say God is our highest priority. Our God-box may even be the biggest of them all. Still, our hearts remain divided into segments that each cry out for gratification.

The LORD does not want just a part of your heart. Jesus wants to break out of the God-box where you confined Him to fill every compartment. However, Jesus won't force His way into rooms you have closed. He will knock at the doors of your heart, but you must choose to open each door and let Him in.

While dead faith keeps the doors of our hearts locked, resurrected faith gives Jesus the keys with unlimited access to every area of our hearts. Living faith removes the dividing line between the sacred and secular to impact all aspects of our lives.

For instance, in my book, *Finding Financial Freedom,* I share six big ideas to help people break free from the bondage of debt. The first is to realize, "Every financial decision is a spiritual issue."[6] Big and small purchases take on a whole new meaning when we erase the line between faith and finances. Living faith opens our eyes to understand how the use of every dollar determines who the owner is. Either we control all our money and possessions or submit to God's ownership of everything we have to serve the LORD as a faithful steward.

The discovery of your singular heart's cry is the first step Jesus wants you to take toward resurrected faith. When we clear away the inner voices and distractions shouting for our attention, we are in a place to be revived by the LORD. We need to hear the psalmist's song to "Be still, and know that I am God" (Psa. 46:10).

Will you take time to stop all the relentless activity of day to day life and listen for Jesus to reveal a singular heart's cry just for you?

I've discovered many people express their heart's cry using a life verse, a scripture with significant meaning to them. Some shared with me how the LORD'S words, *"I know the plans I have for you…to give you a future and a hope,"* from Jeremiah 29:11 strengthens their faith and gives them courage in times of uncertainty. Others look to Isaiah 30:21, *"This is the way, walk in it"* or Philippians 1:6, that *"He who began a good work in you will bring it to completion at the day of Jesus Christ."* The passion that motivates me echoes Jude's ancient heart cry *"to earnestly contend for the faith"* (KJV).

Regardless of the scripture an individual chooses, I listen for two things when I talk with people about the passion that drives them. These two things are the LORD'S desire for each of us. First, and more than anything else, Jesus wants to reveal Himself to us so we can know the God who loves us. Second, Jesus wants to empower and use us to share God's love with others.

The ultimate cry of our hearts should, in some way, simply say, "I want to know Jesus and make Him known."

The Cry for Resurrected Faith

The willingness to acknowledge our faith is dead and in need of resurrection is not natural. We find it easier to pretend everything is okay. With a repeated charade, we deceive our hearts just as Jesus said to the church at Sardis, "You have a reputation of being alive, but you are dead" (Rev. 3:1).

If we are willing to admit the truth, the Holy Spirit will put a relentless desire in our hearts for our faith to be revived. We will cry out to God for dead faith to come alive again.

Jesus will respond to the deep spiritual thirst for resurrected faith. He will come to restore us with the living water of His Spirit.[7]

Nearly two millennia have now passed since Jude wrote his short letter. For those with ears to hear today, the Spirit is calling out for us "to contend for the faith." The plea is urgent. Now is the time to strive for a resurrected faith. "The faith" Jesus revealed and entrusted once and for all to His children is what we desperately need today.

We need to rediscover the faith that is alive. Now is the time to return to Jesus and struggle for a resurrection of faith. Like those in hospice care fighting for their lives, we need our faith to come alive again.

In the *Resurrected Faith* series, we will ask the Holy Spirit to teach us what it means to fight for our faith to come alive again. We take the all-important first step with a heart cry for resurrected faith in our lives, families, churches, and communities.

The focus of book one, *The Heart of a Contender,* is not a quest for more information. We have much to learn about resurrected faith, and the companion study guide will help you apply these truths. However, don't allow your head to push ahead of your heart.

Remember, God initially speaks to our hearts because this is where transformation begins. The Holy Spirit then instructs our minds to strengthen the life of faith first written upon our hearts. Head knowledge without the spark of resurrection power in our hearts is useless.

Perhaps you feel like the hospice patient with life ebbing away. You believe all the right things, but your hope often gives way to anxiety and fear. The joy of life is lost in your day to day routine. While you try to do all the right things—you attend church, read your bible, listen to Christian music, pray, and more—ultimately, you and the hospice patient are powerless to make yourself come alive again.

Intellectual faith alone can be overwhelmed by the circumstances of life. While head knowledge brings about much needed spiritual formation, it cannot transform.

Only the LORD can make us live again with His resurrection power. Just as Jesus can touch the hospice patient and restore the fullness of life in a moment, so, too, the Holy Spirit resurrects faith within our hearts. The Spirit's touch instantly causes endurance, hope, love, joy, peace, wisdom, and more to come alive again.

The heart of a contender cries out to God for resurrected faith. With ever-growing confidence, contenders stand with an assurance that what was dead will live again. The contender's passion yearns with a singular focus to know Jesus and make Him known.

The chapters that follow will help ignite that flame:

- **"A Crisis of Faith"** begins our journey with the call to contend through the activity of *"faithing"* to live what we believe.

- **"The Symptoms of Dead Faith"** reveals our infection with a common sickness only cured by an intimate knowledge of Jesus and the first faith He reveals.

- **"Contenders of the Faith"** present the urgent need not to give in to cultural relativism but struggle for the absolute and singular truth, a doctrine progressively revealed by God since creation and perfectly fulfilled in Jesus.

- **"Don't Be Fooled"** warns how the master of deception wants to keep us from joining the fight for the faith "once for all delivered to the saints."

- **"The Contender's Identity"** encourages us to find rest from our tiresome effort to be somebody in the knowledge we are the adored, protected, and chosen of God.

- **"Unfailing Confidence"** empowers us to live what we believe through the multiplied certainty of God's mercy, peace, and love.

- **"The Heart of a Contender"** shows us how the activity of *"faithing"* aligns our belief and lifestyle, creating a passion to know and defend Jesus, the cornerstone of all we believe.

Resurrected faith is the answer to our prayers.

I'm grateful you have heard the Spirit's call "to contend for the faith." We stand together with believers who yearn for our faith to come alive. You may still cherish a life verse to describe your life's purpose differently, but it will be shaped by a singular heart's cry for Jesus to breathe the breath of life upon what is dead and dying within us.

Only a miracle will bring Jesus' Church, separated by the doctrines and traditions of man into countless denominations, back together with resurrected faith. But this is precisely what Jesus wants to do—to restore the faith He first gave beginning at creation to all who believe. Today, His Spirit prepares us as one Bride that "has made herself ready… adorned for her husband" (Rev. 19:7; 21:2).

We desperately need the Spirit to help us "contend for the faith" because Jesus is coming soon. Raise your voice with the heart cry of a contender for the life of Christ to revive what is dead. Join me in prayer, asking the LORD to help us build bridges of love in place of the divisive doctrinal walls that separate our churches.

Resurrected faith is the answer to our prayers.

Contending for Resurrected Faith

✞ A pandemic of dead faith with eternal consequences threatens our families, churches, and communities.

    o Dead faith knows no boundaries and impacts believers of all Christian denominations.

    o The Holy Spirit wants to awaken us to the dead faith in our lives so we will come to Jesus, who takes what is dead and makes it alive again.

✞ Life-defining moments are memorials of God's transformational power at work in our lives.

✞ Living faith puts a passion into our hearts "to contend for the faith that was once for all delivered to the saints."

✞ Dead faith is a roadblock to the pursuit of a singular heart's cry.

    o We follow the cries within our hearts to find fulfillment in things we yearn for in life.

    o The three C's of your checkbook, calendar, and cares will help you identify the things your heart desires most.

✞ Jesus wants to break out of your God-box to fill every area of your heart.

    o Living faith removes the dividing lines that segregate our hearts.

✝ Jesus wants to give us a singular heart's cry so we will fight for resurrected faith.

Notes: Chapter 1 "A Singular Heart's Cry"

[1] Linnane, Ciara "Coronavirus tally one year on: Golbal cases of COVID-19 top 118 million and U.S. nears 530,000 fatalities." Market Watch. (2021). Accessed March 27, 2021. https://www.marketwatch.com/story/coronavirus-tally-one-year-on-global-cases-of-COVID-19-top-118-million-and-us-nears-530000-fatalities-2021-03-11

[2] LORD – Throughout this book you will see LORD printed with all caps as a reminder of who Jesus is. See introduction note for more.

[3] "Moravian Slaves." Wikipedia. (October, 4 2016), Accessed December 1, 2017. https://en.wikipedia.org/wiki/Moravian_slaves

[4] Jude 1:3 will be quoted in part throughout this book. The scripture reference will only be included when the verse is used in its entirety. Unless otherwise noted quotations from this verse will be from the English Standard Version of the Bible.

[5] Lexicon :: Strong's G75 - Agōnizomai. "Outline of Biblical Usage." BlueLetterBible.org. Accessed March, 14 2018. https://www.blueletterbible.org/lang/lexicon/lexicon.cfm?strongs=G75&t=ESV

[6] Ebie, D. Greg. *Finding Financial Freedom: Your Key to Debt Free Living.* Windham, OH: Firm Foundation Publishing. 2018. p. 13.

[7] See John 7:38-39.

Chapter 2

A Crisis of Faith

I want you to remember the Good News I brought to you. You received this Good News and continue strong in it. And you are being saved by it if you continue believing what I told you. If you do not, then you believed for nothing.

1 Corinthians 15:1-2, NCV

When something is dead within you, take action to have it removed. Otherwise, you will die.

After a not-so-routine surgery to remove my gallbladder, the LORD taught me this life lesson in January 2018.

The Holy Spirit used this experience to teach me spiritual truths I knew in my head but not in my heart.

I did my best to study the Bible and rightly handle God's Word. With thirty years of ministry experience preaching weekly sermons and teaching countless Bible studies, one might think I didn't need an individual tutoring session with the Holy Spirit. Socrates' saying is true, "You don't know what you don't know."[1]

In my days of recovery, God took me to school. The LORD showed me how new life with renewed passion and vibrancy has a chance to grow when what is dead is cut out.

What is Faith?

Few Christians today understand what faith is. They settle for a lifeless imitation rather than grasp the full meaning of biblical faith. Jude said he was "compelled to write to you and encourage you to continue struggling for the faith that was entrusted to the saints once and for all" (Jude 1:3, VOICE). Our response to Jude's ancient call requires an accurate comprehension of what faith is, so we contend for the right thing.

Faith is often thought of in one of two ways. The first is a secular view. The world defines faith as any belief one cannot prove. Knowledge is grounded upon what we can measure, observe, and study, while faith is merely an idea accepted by an individual. In this way, people are sometimes said to have blind faith because they believe so-called truths that cannot be known with certainty.

For others, faith is a religious concept of higher ideals or principles. Religious faith does not necessarily have to be Christian but ascribes to a belief in a god or moral and ethical guidelines of right and wrong. Faith is the creed or doctrine an individual chooses to embrace that may or may not have a lasting impact on their daily lives.

As a believer, you may hold one of these views or some combination of the two. You believe in one God and His only begotten Son, Jesus, the Savior of the world. You accept the Bible as God's Word, the only reliable instruction in righteousness. While you believe all the right things, your ideals and doctrines remain but one choice among countless unprovable opinions.

As we will see, faith acts within our hearts to change us from the inside out, so we live what we believe—faith is a verb.

A Resurrection of Simple Truth

Biblical faith is far more than a belief in Jesus. Beyond guidelines for right living or religious teaching about God, biblical faith is transformative and alive with resurrection power. As we will see, faith acts within our hearts to change us from the inside out, so we live what we believe—faith is a verb.

In the Old Testament, the idea of faith originates in a Hebrew verb and nouns formed by it. The Jewish understanding of faith comes from a verb literally meaning "to support."[2] These words are translated into the KJV of the Bible by more than twenty-five different English words, including believe, established, faith, faithful, faithfulness, father, bring up, nurse, steadfast, sure, trust, truth, truly, verified, and assurance. The variety of ways they are translated in modern versions of the Bible only increases to show the depth of meaning within the concept of faith.

Like an artist's pallet with distinctive colors blended and put on a canvas to create a work of art, a single word cannot capture the Jewish understanding of faith. And as one's appreciation for a work of art grows by carefully looking at it, so through study, we also develop a greater appreciation of what it means to believe and be a person of faith.

To comprehend the rich meaning of faith, we first need to know how Jewish people think. Hebrew and eastern thought is concrete, based upon verbs and action, while our American and western culture tends to be more abstract with nouns and adjectives.

We would define a car with a description as an automobile, vehicle, or a train's boxcar. For example, we describe the color, year, and make of a car by saying something like, "I have a red '95 Ford Mustang." Eastern thought would focus instead on the function or purpose of a car and say, "An automobile takes people from one place to another."

Faith is grounded in the idea "to support" and is best illustrated by Isaiah 22:23, "I will fasten him like a peg in a secure place." The verb for faith is translated here as "secure place." Rather than sandy soil, firm ground is the place chosen to set up a tent. In this way, tent pegs are driven into a solid foundation "to support" the tent against even the strongest winds and faithfully uphold it to stand and not collapse.[3]

The first use of this verb is in Genesis 15:6, but it is translated differently. Abram "believed the LORD, and He counted it to him as righteousness." We understand how Abram had faith in God's word, but to think Abram "supported the LORD" is a foreign idea for us.

How could Abram have faith to make certain, steadfast, and sure an all-powerful God, and what does it mean for you and me to have faith that supports the LORD today?

Faith means more than knowing God exists or having confidence God will do what He says according to His word. To believe with faith produces a resolution to support and uphold the LORD'S will.[4] Abram acted like a tent peg driven by God into the ground. Because Abram believed, he lived his life by faith in complete agreement with God to firmly support what the LORD promised.

Resurrected faith drives us into the solid ground of God's word to hear and obey—the activity of faith transforms us to live what we believe. On the other hand, dead faith is unstable ground with no support to uphold God's word in our lives.

Faith Remains the Same

As we turn the page from Malachi to Matthew in our Bibles, we cannot ignore centuries of Jewish teaching about faith. The activity of faith in the lives of believers was not a new idea. The dynamic of belief "to support" was foundational to what early Christians and New Testament writers thought about faith. Rather than invent the concept of Christian faith or belief, authors like Paul, Peter, James, and John quoted the Old Testament to support what they wrote.

The LORD revealed Himself to His people through the sacred text known to first century Jews and Christians as the Law and the Prophets. They studied Genesis through Malachi as their Holy Bible

> *Resurrected faith is the truth known deep within your "knower" to shape the kind of person you are.*

to know God. Within these Scriptures, they found Jesus and made Him known.

God knew what He was doing when He chose the original languages for His written word. In both Hebrew and Greek, the concept of faith *originates as a verb*. Faith was not static or motionless, waiting for someone or something to act upon it. From Genesis to Revelation, biblical faith is alive and active by the power of the Holy Spirit.

Today, faith remains unchanged. Belief in Christ continues to work vigorously with resurrection power to transform the lives of all who believe, and this activity of faith remains the heart of the gospel message.

Like Hebrew, the concept of faith in Greek originates from a root verb meaning to persuade or be persuaded with confidence to believe, obey, or trust.[5] This word is the parent to the interrelated synonyms "faith," "belief," and "believe."[6] In the first century, Greek was the common language, so people understood how faith or belief was tied to the idea of being persuaded.

In the New Testament, faith implied far more than the modern idea of someone's opinion about so-called relative truth—an opinion with no power to transform. Instead, just like Old Testament faith acted "to support," the activity of New Testament faith convinced an individual to believe with unwavering conviction. First century believers understood how the work of faith transformed the hearts and minds of those who believe by the power of the Holy Spirit.

Unfortunately, our understanding is incomplete because we only think of faith as a noun. Today, faith is generally only thought of as a thing, a concept, or an idea to hold in one's mind. Beliefs are something individuals possess and not considered as acting to change a person from the inside out. We lost the idea that faith is active as a verb. Through the gospel, the Spirit "persuaded" us to believe, so our thinking is renewed by the activity of faith "to support" God's word through obedience.

Just like Abraham "*believed God,* and it was counted to him as righteousness," so too, everyone who believes is saved by faith and not by works (Rom. 4:3 and James 2:23, emphasis mine). You and I are powerless to transform ourselves or live the righteous life God desires. But by faith, the Holy Spirit will revolutionize our lives so we can live what we believe.

Resurrected faith is the truth known deep within your "knower" to shape the kind of person you are. With living faith, God declares the unrighteous sinner to be a righteous saint with living faith.

"Faithing" – The Intersection of Faith to Live What We Believe

We need a change in our thinking to understand faith as *"faithing,"* an intersection of faith to work within us as a noun and a verb, so we live what we believe.

The underlying cause of the crisis of dead faith in the church today is our misunderstanding of faith's activity within us. Our

25

problem rests in our inability to comprehend the fullness of what faith means. We don't think of faith as a verb, working within us to transform our lives from the inside out.

Hebrews 11:1 is the simplest definition of faith in the Bible, "Now faith is the assurance of things hoped for, the conviction of things not seen." We are most familiar with this kind of faith. In this way, the noun of faith shows our confidence and trust in God. However, we are the ones who act wholeheartedly in faith to believe rather than the activity of faith to work within us.

The writer of Hebrews shows us how faith must be more than the noun of our belief. Faith must be *"faithing."* The hope and conviction of faith are necessary because "without faith [noun] it is impossible to please Him, for whoever would draw near to God must believe [faith as a verb] that He exists" (Heb. 11:6). The activity of faith or *"faithing,"* used as both a noun and a verb, is what pleases God.

We understand this in a limited way with the English words belief and believe, a noun and a verb. However, the focus of what we believe is on what we do—we act in faith. As we will see, *"faithing"* is something else.

Simple believing faith is not what Jude urged us to contend for— faith means far more than what we in faith believe or trust God to do for us.

Scripture also uses the word faith as doctrine and teaching— another noun definition. Doctrine is "the substance of Christian faith or what is believed."[7] In this way, faith serves as the foundation of what we believe about God and biblical truth.[8]

Throughout this book, the word faith, the phrase the first faith, or the quotation from Jude 1:3, "the faith" will always refer to the idea of doctrine, the essence of biblical teaching, and not a personal assurance or trusting faith in God. Our recognition of this distinction is the starting place for us to grasp what Jude urges us to go after. "To contend the faith" engages us in a lifetime struggle to know Jesus and the first faith He gave once for all.

"Faithing" or the activity of faith is not something we do. Rather faith or doctrinal truth is alive and active within us through the power of the Holy Spirit. The Spirit fuels faith with absolute truth to do its work, and *"faithing"* is activated to transform us from the inside out, so we live what we believe. Faith is not a work done by us but is a work of the Spirit because "faith comes from hearing, and hearing through the word of Christ" (Rom. 10:17).

Consider this like the software of a computer. The programming and code of this world fill our minds, but the Spirit begins the work of *"faithing"* by writing God's program on our hard drives. The more the truth of God's word we hear, the more the world's destructive programming is rewritten by the activity of *"faithing"* within us. In this way, the work of faith begins transforming the output of how we think, talk, and act. *"Faithing"* makes this change of thinking to persuade us to know Jesus, who is the truth, so that we might believe and be saved.

In time, the activity of faith enables us to come to Jesus with saving faith. Salvation brings a complete transformation to our mainframe and makes us alive in Christ. We receive a new hard drive with God's program written on it—the Holy Spirit makes us "a new creation" (2 Cor. 5:17). Jesus becomes our operating system to direct every area of our lives rather than an app we look to from time to time. When we believe and confess Jesus as LORD, *"faithing"* continues its work to daily reformat our lives, making us more and more like Jesus.

If Jude could speak directly to us today, he would further urge us to contend for resurrected faith. Living active faith goes beyond the head knowledge and biblical doctrine taught in our churches. Faith is not lifeless information to fill our bookshelves or hard drives. Resurrected faith deepens intimacy with Jesus to know Him as He is—head knowledge becomes heart knowledge.

We need a faith resurrection "to contend for the faith" so *"faithing"* can continue its work within us.

Resurrected faith is the working together of faith and belief—both as the noun and the verb as seen in Hebrews 11:6. This *"faithing"* knowledge impacts everything we do and say. Today's missing ingredient in resurrected faith is the first faith—the substance of doctrinal faith and absolute truth given to us by Jesus.

The first faith is resurrected faith—a living faith to transform our lives from the inside out.

A Teachable Moment

My doctor's usual hour-long laparoscopic procedure to remove my gallbladder became a major surgery nearly four hours long. The next day my doctor told me, "Your gallbladder was one of the worst I have ever seen. It was covered with adhesions and a large abscess filled with infection. It was dead."

When you spend five days in the hospital and another week recovering at home, you have lots of time on your hands. I chose to reflect on the events of my illness and surgery. In quiet contemplation, I was reminded of a statement made by Rev. Martha Tennison in many of her sermons, "It's always quiet during surgery. Do you notice how quiet it is now?" In these moments, the Holy Spirit began to teach me some unexpected lessons.

My doctor's words echoed in my mind, *"Something inside me was dead."* This realization stirred still deeper thoughts.

I found myself in a private, teachable moment as the LORD unfolded my personal parable. The Holy Spirit spoke clearly to instruct me about my dead faith. God also showed me how my condition was not unique. Lifeless belief infected countless other believers as well.

You may have heard people say, "God will never put you through more than you can handle." Nice words when you want to encourage those going through hard times. Some people will even validate such a statement with their personal "I overcame" testimony. While their intentions are good, their cliché assurances are simply not true. How would our trusting faith grow stronger if God never allowed us to go through situations we could not handle?

We make it through difficult times because resurrected faith empowers us to persevere and not give up. Living faith brings a peaceful assurance and enables us to rest in the knowledge that our weakness is held securely in the strength of the LORD. You, too, have undoubtedly experienced your share of unwanted hardship—the LORD did not allow these things to crush you. God's purpose is to teach us to rely on His grace during our time of trouble.[9]

James tells us, "as the body apart from the spirit is dead, so also faith apart from works is dead" (James 2:26). The Holy Spirit showed me James was not simply referring to believing faith. Instead, I saw

29

The time is now to awaken with resurrected faith from the plague of dead faith within the Church.

how the substance of our faith is also dead without works. The stuff of faith—the revelation of Jesus, doctrine, and the teaching of Scripture—our belief in these things should be demonstrated daily by how we live our lives.

A transformed life is one way we know our faith is authentic. Consider the Gentile Cornelius. Scripture tells us he was "a devout man who feared God with all his household, gave alms generously to the people, and prayed continually to God" (Acts 10:2).

What made him this way? Some might say it was his faith in God. Yet, at that moment, Cornelius and his household did not have saving faith in God through Jesus Christ. Peter came to preach the gospel and explain its meaning. Instead, even as a non-Jew, Cornelius had been taught about the one true God, *Yahweh*. Cornelius's doctrine or faith changed how he lived daily with the fear of God expressed through generosity and prayer.

Like Cornelius, many Christians do lots of good things but feel empty and spiritually lifeless. When their internal barometer points to a lack of purpose and meaningless works, it might indicate they did those things for the wrong reasons. We long for something more in moments like these, but we are unsure of what it is or how to find it. Our spirits yearn to live according to the truth of the first faith, but we continue a routine of lifeless religious duty.

The Holy Spirit wants to fill our emptiness with resurrected faith—to transform our hearts through the faith we embrace and hold as true. Just as He did with Cornelius, God will make the authentic doctrine and teaching of Scripture come alive within us. Only the power of God can take individual head knowledge and inscribe it on the tablet of our hearts. Faith comes alive when what we believe moves from our heads to our hearts. The Spirit causes our doctrine to impact our desires and change how we live our lives.

How will you respond to the Spirit's conviction concerning the crisis of faith and deadly pandemic that threatens us all?

Don't ignore the problem. Don't believe the lie that dead faith is only someone else's spiritual illness. No one is immune because the plague is everywhere. We have all been infected. In the next chapter, we will look carefully at my personal parable to discover the symptoms of dead faith that infect our hearts and lives.

To make generalities is far easier than to admit you have a sickness only Jesus can heal. The time is now for you and me to awaken with resurrected faith to the plague of dead faith within the Church.

Contending for Resurrected Faith

✝ Today, the Holy Spirit calls believers living in the last days "to contend for the faith."

  o The struggle to know the truth must be engaged with resurrected faith.

  o Our starting place is to comprehend what faith actually is, so we contend for the right thing.

✝ The concept of faith originates as the Hebrew verb *'āman*, which means "to support."

  o To believe with faith transforms how we live our lives, so we act with firmness to support God's word.

✝ The function of faith is belief; it can be expressed in ways such as abiding, confident, persevering, saving, or trusting faith.

✝ The foundation of faith refers to the teaching and doctrine revealed in Jesus Christ our LORD who established the faith once and for all.

✝ The activity of "faithing," the intersection of faith as a noun and a verb, is what pleases God.

  o *"Faithing"* is not something we do but is the work of the Holy Spirit to bring the truth of what we believe to life.

  o Resurrected faith transforms our lives from the inside out to show our belief is genuine by how we live.

✟ No one is immune from the pandemic of dead faith that threatens our lives.

Notes Chapter 2 "A Crisis of Faith"

1 Socrates. AZ Quotes Accessed June 19,2019.. https://www.azquotes.com/qu ote/929533

2 The concept of faith begins in the Old Testament with the verb *'āman* and the nouns *'ēmûn* and *'ĕmûnâ* formed from it. Lexicon:: Strong's H539 - *'āman*. BlueLetterBible.org. Accessed March 28, 2021. https://www.blueletterbible.org/ lang/lexicon/lexicon.cfm?strongs=H539&t=ESV. Lexicon :: Strong's H529 - *'ēmûn*. https://www.blueletterbible.org/lang/lexicon/lexicon.cfm?strongs=H529&t=ESV. Lexicon:: Strong's H530 - *'ĕmûnâ*. https://www.blueletterbible.org/lang/lexicon/ lexicon.cfm?strongs=H530&t=ESV

3 Benner, Jeff A. *The Living Words, Volume One*. College Station, TX: Virtualbookworm.com Publishing Inc. 2007. p. 86.

4 Benner, Jeff A. *Ancient Hebrew Dictionary*. College Station, TX: Virtualbookworm.com Publishing Inc. 2009. p. 74.

5 The verb *peithō* is the basis of faith in the New Testament. Lexicon :: Strong's G3982 – *peithō*. BlueLetterBible.org. Accessed March 28, 2021. https://www.blue letterbible.org/lang/lexicon/lexicon.cfm?page=1&strongs=G3982&t=ESV#lexResults

6 The verb *peithō* is the parent to the noun *pistis* and the verb form *pisteuō*, which together are the synonyms of faith and belief/believe. Lexicon :: Strong's G4100 – *pisteuō*. Accessed March 28, 2021. https://www.blueletterbible.org/lang/lexicon/ lexicon.cfm?Strongs=G4100&t=ESV. Lexicon :: Strong's G4102 – *pistis*. https://www. blueletterbible.org/lang/lexicon/lexicon.cfm?strongs=G4102&t=ESV.

7 Lexicon :: Strong's G4102 – *pistis*. See Thayer's Greek Lexicon.

8 Regarding faith used as doctrine or teaching, Paul's prayer was for believers to obtain *"unity of the faith and of the knowledge of the Son of God"* (Eph. 4:13). He encouraged the Colossians to remain *"established in the faith, just as you were taught"* (Col. 2:7). Timothy had been *"trained in the words of the faith and of the good doctrine"* (1 Tim. 4:6).

9 See 2 Corinthians 12:9.

Chapter 3

The Symptoms of Dead Faith

*His powerful Word is sharp as a surgeon's
scalpel, cutting through everything, whether doubt
or defense, laying us open to listen and obey.*

Hebrews 4:12, MSGB

Something within me was dead. That thought continued to run through my mind. If my gallbladder had not been removed, it would have continued to poison my body. Left untreated, I would die from the infection. The Holy Spirit used my physical sickness and surgery as a personal parable to teach me some important lessons.

The pandemic of dead faith threatens all believers until they are willing to come to the LORD and be healed.

The LORD wants to open our eyes to see the spiritual sickness threatening our lives. Only Jesus can use the scalpel of God's word to cut out the toxic disease of dead faith within the hearts of countless believers today. Unfortunately, too many Christians only deal with the symptoms rather than ask Doctor Jesus to remove the source of the sickness to be healed.

Don't misunderstand. My saving faith was alive and effective. However, just as my dead gallbladder was a small part impacting my entire body, I realized a portion of my faith was dead.

The doctrines I believed produced no lasting works or evidence of life by what I said and did because they were not aligned with the first faith "once for all delivered to the saints." How fervently I believed what my church taught me growing up mattered very little. Misaligned doctrines and the traditions of men only produce dead faith because they lack the power of Christ's resurrected life.

Jude wanted to write "about our common salvation." The gospel points to humanity's common sickness. Sin is a disease only Jesus can cure. In the same way, the pandemic of dead faith threatens all believers until they are willing to come to the LORD and be healed.

Spiritual truth can be a hard pill for any of us to swallow, especially when it is contrary to our accepted beliefs. Little wonder Jeremiah told us how the heart is more deceitful than anything else and beyond human understanding.[1] Now is the time for us to stop lying to ourselves about the dead faith that poisons our hearts. The needed spiritual medicine for resurrection within is available to anyone willing to accept Jesus' diagnosis.

The Symptom of Pain

The first symptom I noticed with my gallbladder was pain. A relentless ache woke me up hours before sunrise like a stab through my back. The pain kept me awake, and the intensity grew stronger as the day wore on.

The trouble, however, began long before the intense pain awakened me. I had dismissed some of the early warning minor pains in my abdomen. Ignoring my discomfort allowed the infection to grow, and my gallbladder to eventually died.

Pain makes us aware of a problem and awakens us to the need to take action. Although the purpose of pain is good, no one likes pain, and we will often seek to avoid it whenever possible.

The pain caused by dead faith is a constant ache often ignored. The irritation may start small, a discomfort you might be tempted to dismiss. But the spiritual pain of dead faith remains. Days without joy, a hunger for the abundant life Jesus promised, or an empty feeling of going through the religious motions are only a few of the ways our spirits begin to ache within us.

Don't ignore your pain.

For me, the ache in my spirit was a simple longing for more. More joy and peace. More contentment. More fruitfulness—an effective witness, combined with answered prayer. The continual longing and dissatisfaction within me created a spiritual numbness, so I ignored my pain. But the poison of dead faith grew stronger until the Holy Spirit awakened me with a pain that I could no longer soothe or overlook.

You have felt it, too, haven't you? If you resist the idea that your faith is dead, you've ignored the purpose of this ache in your heart. Scripture tells us, "all discipline seems painful rather than pleasant, but later it yields the peaceful fruit of righteousness to those who have been trained by it" (Heb. 12:11). The Greek word translated "discipline" can also mean instruction.[2] The Holy Spirit wants to teach us the truth about ourselves and the faith we hold so dear.

We each have some dead faith in our hearts. The presence of lifeless belief does not mean we do not have saving faith. If we confess Jesus is our LORD and believe God raised Christ from the dead, we are saved. The issue is not our salvation. Instead, the question is whether or not we have good works prepared by God to accompany the faith and doctrine we believe.[3]

Resurrected faith responds to the pain with *"faithing."* Living faith will not numbly continue the routine of life but will look to Jesus to help us do the work needed to change the way we live.

The Symptom of "Wrong Places"

With an awareness of pain, I looked for a cure. The first place I looked was the medicine cabinet at home. Nothing there worked, and the pain only intensified. Susie took me to an urgent care center. After waiting over an hour, the doctor didn't even examine me. He said, "I can't help you here. You need to go to the emergency room at the main hospital for treatment." Two wrong places with no relief for the

40

unrelenting pain that was, like a knife, stabbing through my back and stomach.

In one way or another, we all look in the wrong places for a cure for our spiritual pain.

Sometimes Christians do this is by church hopping. When one experiences difficulties in a local church, it's easier to leave than to work through the pain of conflict to find the cause and, in turn, the needed cure. Unresolved conflict in our lives points to the symptom of looking in the wrong places.

We make a mistake and think the local church is the problem—the issue is either the pastor or the people there and not with us. So, we decide to go to worship someplace else. Unfortunately, we fail to realize we are carrying our part in the sickness with us.

When we look for a cure in the wrong place, we forget that God has not called us to switch churches, but to bear "with one another in love, eager to maintain the unity of the Spirit in the bond of peace" (Eph. 4:2-3). Jesus wants us to learn to work through our issues with mercy and kindness rather than run away and ignore the problem.

Another way we look for the cure in the wrong place is to shift the blame. Sometimes we may compare ourselves with others and believe the lie that our spiritual sickness is not that bad. The scriptures teach us that when we measure ourselves with each other, we "are without understanding" (2 Cor. 10:12).

At other times we are quick to blame the devil for the trouble we experience within our lives and the church. In April 2016, our church family at Life Church experienced an unexpected schism. Over the next few months, nearly 40-percent of the congregation chose to leave. After this split, people told me again and again:

- "Pastor, we're not going to let Satan win."
- "The devil is trying to destroy our church, but we won't let him."
- "I'm praying for you, Pastor, so you won't be discouraged by this attack of the enemy."
- "Pastor, God is on our side, and we will overcome."

These people meant well, and for a while, I agreed with them. But the Holy Spirit helped me understand we had shifted the blame and were looking in the wrong places.

We have a real enemy—"our adversary the devil prowls around like a roaring lion, seeking someone to devour" (1 Peter 5:8). The devil specializes in death and destruction. However, the scriptures also teach us "it is for discipline that you have to endure. God is treating you as sons" (Heb. 12:7). Sometimes we need to look in the mirror rather than blame the devil for our trouble.

Looking in the wrong places by running away through unresolved conflict or shifting blame away from ourselves is a common problem for the spiritual ache in our hearts.

To find the cure for the pain, we must stop looking in the wrong places. With resurrected faith, the Spirit can help us look deep within and examine the condition of our hearts. Ask God to give you the insight to look in the right places.

You and I are not doctors trained to diagnose the deadly problem in others, nor are we capable of treating the disease that threatens our lives. Instead, we are patients with a growing pain in desperate need of a cure. Jesus is the Great Physician and has the medication we need. But, the necessary treatment won't be available until we acknowledge the disease of dead faith as our real problem.

Living faith looks in the right places to deal with the pain of indifferent religious beliefs. With resurrected faith, the Holy Spirit will help us to stop looking in the wrong places. Ask God to give you the wisdom to look in the right places.

The Symptom of Medication Denial

Late Friday afternoon, about two hours after going to the emergency room, the attending physician diagnosed my problem. He ordered pain medication more potent than anything in my medicine cabinet at home, and at long last, I had some relief.

He told me, "You can have emergency surgery tonight, or you can wait to schedule the procedure with a surgeon on Monday." Surgery was not on my bucket list of things to do, so I opted for the latter. Besides, I did not have time for surgery because of the ministry commitments I needed to keep. The doctor sent me home with pain medication enabling me to go ahead with my plans for the weekend.

The proper medication can stop the pain. With the help of a few pain pills, my restless discomfort was gone, but the cause remained. I went through the weekend in denial of my dying gallbladder.

Many believers are over-medicated to dull their awareness of the pain caused by their dead faith. We have developed various spiritual pills to numb the pain while the source of our spiritual illness lingers unchecked.

A favorite spiritual narcotic is an endless lineup of activity—we are always busy. With work, school, family, community, church, and other events, we have no shortage of things to do. Even when our schedule has a break, we fill our time with entertainment or hobbies—anything to keep us from being still and feeling the pain of dead faith.

The most potent of these medications to inoculate us from the pain of dead faith is ministry activity. Involvement in our churches or other ministry functions does not mean we don't have dead faith. Our spiritual endeavors only help us to numb the pain, so we don't notice it. Even if you're not involved with a local church, it is easy to fill our lives with the activity of other good works to anesthetize our consciences.

Ministry and service within our church and community are important. But if we are not careful, our deeds can be used to medicate our dead faith and justify all the busy activity that we claim to do for the LORD.

The pain of dead faith makes us like Martha, busy with the work of ministry but not sitting in Jesus' presence to simply know Him more. Jesus told her, "you are anxious and troubled about many things, but one thing is necessary" (Luke 10:41-42). Her sister Mary chose what was best and necessary. She enjoyed Jesus' presence and simply sat at His feet.

We, too, need to understand what is necessary. A full calendar with ministry and service activities dull the pain of dead faith, but busyness is not the prescription required to cure our sickness. Instead, we need time to stop and just wait in the LORD'S presence. In quiet rest, Jesus will renew our strength and heal us, so we will live and not die.

Resurrected faith refuses to medicate and ignore the pain but is set free from endless activity to spend time with Jesus.

The Symptom of Sticky Adhesions

My doctor explained why they could not perform the routine laparoscopic procedure. "The adhesions on your gallbladder stuck onto living tissue all around it." My dead gallbladder clung tightly to the living tissue hoping to suck the life out of everything it touched.

In much the same way, sticky adhesions cover dead faith making similar attachments in the search for life.

The Holy Spirit taught me when something is dying, it seeks out life wherever it can find it. I had unknowingly done this. As a pastor, my entire life revolved around the people and activities within the church. While I shared the life of Christ with others in the church, I also sucked up as much for myself as I could find, specifically through friendships with others in ministry or gatherings with other pastors at conferences, meetings, and other special events.

Today, many who regularly attend churches do so simply because it is the only attachment they have to the life of Christ. We go to church and suck up as much of this life as we can each Sunday but live the rest of the week in a spiritual wasteland.

Sticky adhesions of dead faith make us a lot like King Saul. After anointing Saul as Israel's future king, Samuel gave Saul a sign that the Spirit of the LORD would come upon him to prophesy among the prophets. When this happened, the people began to ask, "Is Saul among the prophets?" (1 Sam. 10:11).

While Saul enjoyed the recognition of being thought of as someone who was spiritually alive, the sticky adhesions of his dead faith were evident when he disobeyed the LORD'S command to entirely devote the Amalekites to destruction. Saul brought back

Agag, their king, alive together with the best of the livestock. When Samuel asked about all the sheep and oxen, Saul blamed the people with a pretense to sacrifice them for burnt offerings to worship the LORD. Because Saul rebelled and ignored the LORD'S instructions, Samuel told him the LORD likewise rejected him as king.

Saul responded with a half-hearted confession, "Please pardon my sin and return with me that I may bow before the LORD" (1 Sam. 15:25). Notice the symptoms of dead faith in his confession. First, Saul looked in the wrong place for a cure and asked Samuel to forgive his sin rather than come with a contrite heart to the LORD with his request for mercy. Second, Saul wanted the people to see him worship the LORD with Samuel.

Saul's faith in God was not alive, so he clung to Samuel for the appearance of spiritual life. However, Saul revealed the full extent of his dead faith by begging Samuel, "Honor me now before the elders of my people and before Israel, and return with me, that I may bow before the LORD your God" (verse 30). His words revealed his selfish desire to be thought of as spiritually alive in other people's eyes because the LORD was not his God but Samuel's.

In the years that followed, things only went from bad to worse, "the Spirit of the LORD departed from Saul, and a harmful spirit from the LORD tormented him" (1 Sam. 16:14). Saul then found comfort in another sticky adhesion with young David, who, with a heart to seek the LORD, was anointed by Samuel to one day replace Saul as king.

With dead faith, you and I can be a lot like Saul going through the motions of being spiritually alive but disconnected from the source.

When we are intimately connected to Jesus, His joy fills us and causes our joy to overflow.[4] Unfortunately, dead faith dries up our reservoir of rejoicing. Rather than look to Jesus to provide what is needed, lifeless belief seeks out attachments with others to obtain satisfaction from the life of Jesus within them. And when our lives are not flooded with Jesus' joy, worship becomes a hollow routine. Like Saul, our prayers, songs, and activities of worship become little more than a sideshow performance to make us look good in the eyes of others.

Dead faith always seeks out life in the wrong places. The lifelessness within conceals itself through connections with more spiritually alive people. Dead faith remains hidden behind its sticky adhesions, rather than look to Jesus as the source of life.

Resurrected faith, the first faith, is alive. Living faith produces an overflow of adoration and obedience to the LORD Jesus. Living faith makes an intimate connection to the Source and not a substitute. Ask the Holy Spirit to reveal the ways we have fooled ourselves with the illusion of life rather than receiving the abundant life Jesus promised to give us.

Now is time for us to let the Master Surgeon cut us free from our sticky adhesions with resurrected faith that we might be healed and truly live.

The Symptom of Abscessed Infection

The final symptom is an abscess filled with infection that, given enough time, will kill you. Poison filled my gallbladder—if left untreated, it would infect my entire body, and in time, result in my death. Rather than let the surgeon remove it right away, I decided to schedule surgery for a more convenient time, which unknowingly allowed the infection to continue to grow within me.

In the same way, dead faith produces an abscess filled with a deadly spiritual infection. Given enough time, the toxins it carries will kill us. The contamination concealed within our lifeless beliefs is a matter of life and death.

Consider the contrast between the LORD'S response to the wicked and righteous men who forsake their former ways of living. God notices of the sinful man who repents and turns away from his evil deeds. Because this man did not continue a habit of disobedience but by faith turned to walk a path of obedience, God said, "he shall surely live; he shall not die" (Ezek. 18:21). His lifetime of evil would not be remembered because the LORD does not find pleasure in the death of the wicked, but rather that they would repent of their many sins and live.

But what about the righteous person who willfully turned to the evil forsaken by the wicked man? You and I would not want to ignore all the good things done by the righteous man. Unlike God, we consider these deeds to balance or even outweigh the evil he chose. Such a perspective makes salvation the result of works and not by faith.

The LORD saw how the righteous man's faith was dead so that what he believed no longer supported or upheld God's word. The mercy he received became null and void because dead faith caused him to turn away from doing what pleased God. The LORD said, "None of the righteous deeds that he has done shall be remembered; for the treachery of which he is guilty and the sin he has committed, *for them he shall die*" (Ezek. 18: 24, emphasis mine).

48

Like you and me, believers today who ignore the toxins of dead faith are in grave danger. The poison of dead faith slowly infects every area of our lives. In time, we begin to compromise and, step by step, betray the LORD turning away from our righteous deeds. Our sin brings the discomfort of conviction, but the infection of dead faith keeps us from feeling the entire weight of its pain. Rather than ask Jesus to cut away what is dead within us, the pleasures of this world anesthetize our hearts, and we remain unrepentant—unchanged.

Don't be deceived. Dead faith is a deadly virus within our hearts that will eventually kill us.

We are made alive in Christ by God's grace through saving faith. However, this alone is not resurrected faith. Through our knowledge of Christ, *"faithing"* empowers us to follow in His steps. Jesus fulfilled the Law through His complete obedience. For us to live like Jesus means learning how to apply the entirety of scripture to our daily lives.

Unfortunately, the doctrine of some ignores this truth. Rather than try to understand the Old Testament, they teach that by the same grace of God, we are not under the Law, and therefore, we are not obligated to obey it. Such teaching is contrary to the first faith given by the LORD.[5]

One cannot fully know Jesus or comprehend Matthew through Revelation without understanding Genesis to Malachi, the Old Testament law, and prophets.

While resurrected faith teaches us to walk in obedience to all of God's word, Christians today must also be careful not to fall into the other extreme of legalism. Salvation does not come by obedience or works of the Law because "it's by God's grace that you have been

Resurrected faith responds to the deadly infection of dead faith and turns to Jesus to be healed before it is too late.

saved. You receive it through faith. *It was not our plan or our effort. It is God's gift, pure and simple"* (Eph. 2:8, VOICE, emphasis mine). Living faith rests in the work only Jesus can do to save us, while at the same time responding to the inner activity of *"faithing"* to God's word with a life of obedience.

Dead faith responds differently to the truth of God's word. Our lifeless belief makes us do and say things in public to appear righteous. Unfortunately, our religious words and pious deeds are often contradicted in private or when we are with a different crowd.

Dead faith makes us a lot like Ananias and Sapphira in Acts 5. They found out too late that dead faith will kill you—sometimes suddenly. Together they sold a piece of property to help provide for the needs of other believers. They held back some of the proceeds for themselves but brought the rest and laid it at the Apostles' feet—they did this with the pretense they gave everything they received. Peter told Ananias, "You have not lied to man but to God" (Acts 5:4). When he heard this, Ananias fell to the ground, dead. A few hours later, his wife Sapphira stood before Peter, not knowing what had happened. She repeated the lie and, like her husband, fell dead at Peter's feet.

We are sometimes guilty of acting just like Ananias and Sapphira. The Holy Spirit showed me how I sometimes wear an appearance of righteousness before people but privately yield to temptation and sin.

I'm not alone. For Christians to live contrary to what they say they believe is to ignore the infection of dead faith that always leads to sin and death.

The hidden puss of compromise and sin fills the private places of our lives. Such a spiritual abscess causes us to turn away from living each day in righteousness. Faithful obedience in every area of our lives is only possible with resurrected faith—daily living our lives saturated in the life of Jesus.

Resurrected faith responds to the deadly infection of dead faith and turns to Jesus to be healed before it is too late.

The First Faith

Francis Chan begins his book *Crazy Love* by asking François Fénelon's question, "to just read the Bible, attend church, and avoid 'big' sins—is this passionate, wholehearted love for God?" Chan then writes what many Christians understand intuitively: "We all know something's wrong."[6] I agree with Chan because, as he said, "When you are wildly in love with someone, it changes everything."[7]

More than ten years have passed since Chan first wrote those words. I can't help thinking that something is still wrong today. For all the Christian faith has to offer, the lives of many so-called Christians today are not very different from those who don't believe. We still need more of Jesus in our lives, to love Him more and the things of this world less.

We are accustomed to the dead faith within and may wonder if such a love for God is even possible. The longing remains as the Holy Spirit continues to His work to "convict the world concerning sin and righteousness and judgment" (John 16:8). We feel the gentle nudge of the Spirit's conviction and yearn to love Jesus more today than yesterday.

You feel this heartfelt desire for more, too—don't you?

Contending for the first faith is not about struggling to discover a creed or a doctrine. To fall more deeply in love with an idea or religious words is hard, if not impossible. Yes, faith is the substance of belief established and given by Jesus once and for all. However, we do not come to know Jesus through a creed or doctrine that attempts to define Him.

I know it's counterintuitive. Our churches and Christian media overflow with teaching about Jesus, but more information is not enough. Instead, we need greater intimacy with Christ. You and I come to know the first faith and true doctrine simply by knowing and loving Jesus—resurrected faith is found in the life of our LORD.

"To contend for the faith" means we come to know Jesus as He truly is and not as various Church doctrines and traditions have shaped Him over the last 2,000 years.

Jude understood this reality before the first century had passed into history. Already he saw how false teachers had crept into the church to "pervert the grace of our God into sensuality and deny our only Master and LORD, Jesus Christ" (Jude 1:4). These ungodly people were not just distorting the doctrine or teaching held by the Early Church. They were reinventing the person of Jesus to suit their desires.

Contending for the faith means more than exposing false teaching concealed within the doctrines and traditions of man. We cannot bring to light doctrinal error unless we first know the truth. Jesus is the truth, which is not found by contending to gain more knowledge about God. Instead, we struggle to grasp the first faith by knowing and loving Jesus as He truly is.

Remember, don't put your head before your heart. We tend to want to put reason before our relationship with God—we want faith to make sense. However, Jesus always leads His followers through an intimate heart connection and not rational head knowledge.

For now, our purpose is to allow the Holy Spirit to speak to our hearts so we know the truth about ourselves and are not deceived. We will never come to Jesus to be healed until we understand how desperately sick we are. In book two, *Resurrected Faith: Your Passion to Know Jesus the Cornerstone,* we will look at Christ our Cornerstone's unseen and seen realities to more fully comprehend who Jesus is and defend the truth He reveals.

A Crisis of Faith

The Holy Spirit wants to reveal what is dead within us. Awakening to the truth may come through our personal devotions, a sermon, a book we read, or other so-called "spiritual" ways. But, if we listen carefully, the LORD will also use our ordinary day to day life experiences to speak to us. Sometimes these events come as times of crisis and turmoil. God wants to reveal the unseen realities within our hearts during such difficult moments.

The resurrection power of life is far greater than the stronghold of death that seeks to destroy us and our faith. Jesus, the Master Surgeon, can remove the anemic and lifeless belief within us and replace it with living faith.

For years I led our congregation in a simple prayer to prepare our hearts for the preaching of God's Word: "Holy Spirit, empower us to have eyes to see, ears to hear and hearts that are willing to obey Your Word." In those days of unexpected heartache and trial, this prayer reverberated in my heart more and more. Slowly but surely, God answered that prayer for me.

My singular heart's cry and the purpose of *Resurrected Faith* is that we might learn "to contend for the faith that was once for all delivered to the saints." The faith given to us by Jesus is alive. Unlike the dead belief of Christians so widespread today, the first faith is energetic and overflows with life to transform peoples' lives.

Think about the power of life within the faith of first century believers. People were saved daily—miracles of healing took place, and the dead were raised to life. But that's not all. Those bound by demons were set free. Sin within the church was exposed and removed. Their faith was not dead but full of life! Believers within the Early Church, radiant with this living faith, turned their world upside down.

Do we find such evidence of vibrant life within our churches today? If we are honest, we know our faith is lacking. Something is deadly wrong within our churches.

Whatever is poisoned and lifeless today within the church must be removed. Dead faith cannot be ignored. Only with the scalpel of His Word can Jesus cut out the infection within us. You and I cannot cure ourselves. We must come to Jesus. Only He has resurrection power to take what is dead and make it alive again. The first faith is teeming with the life of Jesus.

Believers in the first century were ordinary people just like you and me. Just as they impacted their world some 2,000

What is dead can come alive again.

years ago, we can watch God bring life into our families and neighborhoods through us. Living faith resonating within our churches will overflow to transform our communities with the power of the gospel.

Resurrected faith given by Jesus is what we need today. We are in desperate need of healing. The starting place is for each of us to allow Jesus, the Master Surgeon, to cut away what is dead in us.

Have you, like me, grown tired of going through the motions trying to live out your Christian faith with little or no fruit to show for it? Deep down, we know something is missing. The Holy Spirit places a yearning within our hearts to move beyond the "faith" we are so comfortable with and find something more, something alive.

We need to stop trying to fill the emptiness in our lives with the pleasures of addictions, materialism, social media, streaming videos, and other barren promises of this world. Nor will a *"convenient store Jesus"* as defined by the dead faith doctrine of so many churches today satisfy the longing of our souls either. Unfortunately, the faith within the American Church is lukewarm at best and puts us in danger of being spit from Jesus' mouth.[8]

Jesus calls us to radical discipleship and obedience to His Word. With resurrected faith, we will find the fullness of life only He can give. Now is the time to answer Jesus' call to stop striving with human energy and religious piety.

Now is the time to repent of the dead faith within us and our churches. Surrender to Jesus and ask the Holy Spirit to resurrect our faith because God will answer honest prayers like these. The same power of the Spirit that raised Jesus from the dead is at work today.

What is dead can come alive again.

Contending for Resurrected Faith

✟ We contend with a personal awakening to dead faith within our hearts and lives.

    o   The symptoms of dead faith are often ignored because the heart is deceitful and desperately sick.

✟ Some of the symptoms of pain include a longing for more intimacy with Jesus, more Christlikeness, more fruitfulness, a lack of joy, or an empty feeling of going through religious motions.

✟ The symptoms of wrong places cause believers to hop churches with unresolved conflict or shift the blame to other people and/or the enemy.

✟ Endless family activity, church and community events, good works, and ministry are symptoms of medication denial to numb the pain of dead faith.

✟ The symptom of sticky adhesions suck nourishment from the connections made with other believers rather than intimacy with Jesus the source of life.

✟ The symptoms of dead faith produce a deadly infection, appearing righteous in public, but in private is disobedient, given to sin, and ignores or justifies oneself against the conviction of the Holy Spirit.

✝ Resurrected faith goes beyond a mere doctrine or a creed; it is a personal revelation of Jesus Christ and loving Him as He truly is.

- o Intimate knowledge of who Jesus is defines the first faith entrusted to the saints once and for all.

- o To contend for the first faith guards against allowing the doctrines and traditions of man to define who Jesus is.

Notes: Chapter 3 "The Symptoms of Dead Faith"

[1] See Jeremiah 17:9.

[2] The Greek word *paideia* often translated "discipline" is not intended for punishment but instruction. Lexicon :: Strong's G3809 – *paideia*. https://www.bluelet terbible.org/lang/lexicon/lexicon.cfm?Strongs=G3809&t=ESV

[3] See Romans 10:9-10; Ephesians 2:10.

[4] See John 15:11.

[5] See Romans 6:1-2; 1 John 3:4.

[6] Chan, Francis. *Crazy Love*. Colorado Springs, CO: David C. Cook. 2008, p. 17.

[7] Chan. Back cover.

[8] See Revelation 3:16.

Chapter 4

Contenders of the Faith

*I want to know [the Anointed Jesus] inside and
out. I want to experience the power of His
resurrection and join in His suffering, shaped by
His death, so that I may arrive safely at the
resurrection from the dead.*

Philippians 3:10-11 (VOICE)

A man who stands for nothing will fall for anything. The gullible and naïve are easily fooled like reeds that appear to stand until the wind blows. Contenders are different.

Like warriors in battle, they set their feet with a single-minded resolve not to be moved.

History shows us many examples of those who decided to stand and contend against the opposition, regardless of the cost. Winston Churchill led the British nation to persevere during the ongoing war against the Nazis. The task to hold the lines during the early stages of WWII fell to the British. Many of her allies had succumbed to Hitler's offensive. London was relentlessly bombed for months, but the British refused to surrender.

After standing alone for nearly a year against the Nazis and Axis powers, Churchill made a speech in which he is remembered for saying, "Never, never, never give up." What Churchill actually said was even more powerful and filled with depth of meaning:

> Surely from this period of ten months, this is the lesson: never give in, never give in, never, never, never, never in nothing, great or small, large or petty—never give in except to convictions of honor and good sense. Never yield to force; never yield to the apparently overwhelming might of the enemy.[1]

Churchill rallied the British people to contend against what seemed like overwhelming odds. Never yield to the enemy. Never give in when you feel like giving up. Never yield or surrender except to the moral principles of what is right.

Take A Stand

Centuries earlier, Jude made a similar appeal to engage in a spiritual struggle. He called followers of Jesus "to contend for the faith that was once for all delivered to the saints." Jude urged believers to never, never, never give in—except to the unyielding convictions of their common salvation, the faith once delivered by Jesus. Never yield to the doctrine of false teachers. Never cheapen the grace of God and give in to the pleasures of sin. And never surrender to the apparently overwhelming might of their adversary, the devil.

Sadly, many Christians enjoy this perceived comfort and live day to day unchanged.

Today, the Holy Spirit sounds the alarm for us to engage in the same battle. Now is the time for believers to take a stand and contend for the first faith given by Jesus once and for all.

Contend means "to struggle in opposition," or "to strive in rivalry, compete."[2] Jude used a Greek compound word translated "contend" that carries far more intensity than our simple English understanding. Vine's Expository Dictionary points out the KJV adds "earnestly contend" to convey the dynamic force in the original—we are to contend "as a combatant."[3] The English word agony, which comes from the Greek root word, helps us grasp what it means to engage in the struggle for the faith.[4] Whether one competes in a sport as an athlete, a fight against an adversary, a stand against difficulty and danger, or a battle to obtain something, the zealous act of contending is never easy.

To contend is hard work that can bring physical, emotional, and intellectual agony. Don't make the mistake and think contending for the faith will be easy. "To contend for the faith" is a call to be vigilant and ever aware of those who seek to pervert the truth "once for all delivered to the saints."

More than once, I've learned the hard way how difficult it is to contend spiritually. The devil gets us comfortable and lulls us to sleep. I've been there—unaware of how the routine of going to church and doing the right things becomes monotonous and lifeless. Sadly, many Christians enjoy this perceived comfort and live day to day unchanged. Spiritually numb, they believe Satan's lie, "God has blessed you."

However, I have also experienced the Spirit's awakening in my heart. I've yearned to know Jesus more intimately, to be more like Him. In these moments, a spiritual bombardment begins. When we come under the enemy's attack, we will either retreat again to a complacent Christianity or take a stand to contend with the spiritual energy God gives.

Perhaps you've found yourself on a similar saintly merry-go-round. Isn't it time we get off this endless ride and take a stand for something real—something alive?

Those who choose to contend for the faith are awake. They have answered the Spirit's call. Contenders are those with a wholehearted desire to know Jesus as He truly is. They refuse to accept the lifeless caricatures our various denominations and traditions make Jesus out to be.

Contenders take an uncompromising stand for the truth, which is absolute and unchanging. These spiritual warriors refuse to succumb to the cultural relativism that permeates our world today. They bridge the artificial gulf that separates the secular and sacred because "all truth is God's truth, no matter where it is found."[5] Contenders seek the truth because through it we come to know Jesus more fully, who is Himself "the truth" (John 14:6).

Believing Faith Versus "The Faith"

It's an age-old question: "Which came first, the chicken or the egg?" Contenders have a similar question to consider: "Which came first, our believing faith or 'the faith?'" While intellectually, we may know "the faith" or doctrine came before we believed in God, all too often, we tend to put our personal, trusting faith first.

A subtle but significant difference exists between believing faith in Christ and "the faith" Jude says was established "once for all." Believing faith can be subjective and often pertains to the individual. The first faith is objective and remains steadfast—its trustworthiness is not moved or shaken by one's rollercoaster of feelings, questions, and doubts. Authentic faith is grounded in the unchanging reality of who Jesus is.

Resurrected faith provides an unshakable foundation to stand even when some people reject its truth as unbelievable.

Believing faith can be described as being strong or weak.[6] One's confidence to believe and trust in God can ebb and flow like the oceans' high and low tides. Even one's saving faith may sometimes rise with a bold assurance or fall with an uncertainty of God's amazing grace.

Many Christians put their pastors up on spiritual pedestals regarding faith. Churchgoers consider their pastors mighty in belief,

Resurrected faith provides an unshakable foundation to stand even when some people reject its truth as unbelievable.

an unshakeable man of faith, a woman of God. The truth is, they are ordinary men and women. Doubts and fears with unanswered questions will sometimes overcome pastors, too.

Many times, I have experienced the waning and waxing of my beliefs. I know what it is for my faith to soar like an eagle and fall to the ground like a flightless chicken.

When my sister-in-law Carol went through a year of treatment in 2019 for myelofibrosis, an uncommon type of bone marrow cancer, our faith was strong, confident God would heal her. My wife Susie was a perfect match for the stem cell transplant—the only cure possible. We called Carol *"Hezekily"* after king Hezekiah, whom the LORD said in his sickness, "I will add fifteen years to your life" (Isa. 38:5). With confident faith, I believed God spoke a similar promise saying, "she will live and not die."

When the disease progressed to acute leukemia, and she was hospitalized at the Cleveland Clinic, we daily said, "Hope is around the corner." Her room was only about forty feet down the hall and a right turn into the transplant unit where the cure awaited to save her life.

The doctors warned us about the various reactions caused by the radiation treatments. When Carol's body grew weak, suffering from these side effects, I prayed with authority for her complete healing. Each time, her faith was encouraged, and God renewed her strength.

In January 2020, she developed a blood infection and moved upstairs to the I.C.U. a second time. Again, we prayed, believing this was just another complication God would help her overcome. Over the next twenty-four hours, none of us were prepared for the critical turn of events that suddenly ended her life.

Her death shook my faith to its foundation. Gathered around her bedside and weeping uncontrollably, I said to my wife and family, "I don't understand! This was not how her story was supposed to end."

You have felt your trusting faith falter with questions and doubt, too—haven't you?

Day to day and moment to moment, your faith and mine can be very different. When life is smooth sailing, we feel confident with strong faith to move mountains. When the storms rage, our trusting faith is sometimes lost in the shadow of the mountains we face. God seems distant, and our prayers go unanswered. I'm thankful storms cease, and mountains move not based upon the size of our believing faith but the mighty power and faithfulness of our God.[7]

Jude has something else in mind when he urges us to "contend for the faith." Granted, we can struggle against the enemy to persevere and strengthen our believing faith, but that is not "the faith" Jude is talking about.

"The faith" refers to an absolute eternal unified body of truth revealed by God in the fullness of Jesus. Scripture reinforces the idea of faith as the objective doctrine and teaching we believe in Christ. For example, Luke tells us that the number of disciples increased in Jerusalem, and a large number of priests "became obedient to the faith," and the Apostle Paul wrote how he preached "the faith he once tried to destroy" (Acts 6:7; Gal. 1:23).

To "contend for the faith" is to struggle to know and believe the doctrine given to us by the LORD through the revelation of Jesus Christ from Genesis to Revelation. We will look at this more fully in book two, *Resurrected Faith: Your Passion to Know Jesus the Cornerstone.* For now, simply remember the faith we contend for is grounded in who Jesus is and not the doctrinal statements taught by our various churches.

The first faith—living faith is defined and revealed through an intimate knowledge of Christ because apart from Jesus, "the faith" is unknowable.

The importance of understanding this subtle difference between our believing faith and "the faith" cannot be overstated. While important, our struggle is not for a more confident, stronger trusting faith in God, nor to fight for saving faith in the lives of others. Instead, we must contend for the first faith coming to know the doctrine and substance of what we believe as revealed in the person of Jesus.

Resurrected faith is alive through knowing Jesus more deeply and, in turn, will strengthen our believing trusting faith. Unfortunately, our academic and intellectual study is powerless to produce living belief or resurrected faith. Countless theologians have studied the Bible and considered the life of Jesus through the ages without personally knowing Christ or the first faith.

Religious activity and belief never produce life—only a relationship with the living God can do that. Our faith comes alive when we experience the life, love, and presence of Jesus in our lives. Through personal and corporate worship, prayer, meditation, and study of the Scriptures, the Holy Spirit reveals and makes Jesus and "the faith" more fully known.[8]

One Faith

The heart of a contender has a passion for knowing Jesus more. Our motivation to stand firm is not to win an argument or prove a point. Our desire is for a greater depth of understanding of who Jesus is.

Across the centuries, Jude urges us "to contend earnestly for *the faith*" and not *the faiths* (NKJV emphasis mine). Jude did not encourage first century believers to struggle for multiple beliefs or doctrines but one unified revelation of God.

"The faith" revealed by Jesus is singular and not a faith among many. Unfortunately, as the years passed, the Church split into countless denominations, each with their version of what they call "the faith" or Christian doctrine. Jesus never intended for His Church to believe in different faiths but one.

As believers today, we may not agree on all matters of doctrine. Your faith and mine can be different, but by and large, we all agree on what matters most. Most Christians will not compromise on the divinity of Jesus Christ—He is God in the flesh and the only way of salvation. We may express Jesus being God somewhat differently, but we each recognize one another's doctrine as the foundation of the Christian faith.

On other doctrinal truths, we do not have the same agreement.

For example, the Church of Christ refuses to "play at worship," singing songs a cappella to an audience of One. At the same time, countless other Christian churches use musical instruments of all shapes and sizes in their worship services.[9]

Seventh-day Adventist and Messianic Congregations gather on the Sabbath—Saturday, but most other Christian Churches choose Sunday as the day of worship. Both are ready to defend their choice with scriptural arguments.

The gulf between some Baptist and Pentecostal churches can be as wide and deep as the Grand Canyon. Their differences are debated from eternal security, speaking in tongues, and more, often ignoring their shared belief in Christ as Savior and LORD.

For these and other differences in doctrine, Christians either agree to disagree or, worse, refuse to fellowship with one another. Some even go so far as to question the validity of one another's faith as heretics.

How unfortunate that Christian Churches hold to statements of faith so opposed to each other. The disagreements between the various doctrines cannot coexist, regardless of how small or large our differences may be. No one can believe both "A" and "not-A." Our many contradictions are evidence of how far the Church drifted the first faith Jesus gave us.

To say "the faith" is a lot for us to comprehend is an understatement. So, for a moment, let's simplify the totality of Christian doctrine into the equation $2 + 2 = 4$. We will use this simple mathematical statement to represent the one true faith given by Jesus and for which we all contend. As Christians, we all believe in "4."

Before adding, subtracting, multiplying, or dividing, we learned how to count. We started at one and soon came to four, but how did we know the meaning of the abstract number "4?" Our parents and teachers taught us to count concrete realities in our day to day world. We counted things like apples, blocks, or crayons. In time, we not only learned what "4" is, but we also could distinguish it from things that were not "4."

The same is true for the first faith. You and I came to know Jesus through elementary truths step by step. Eventually, we began to grasp the simple reality *"Jesus loves me, this I know; for the Bible tells me so."*

Regardless of our age, we come to know Jesus with this kind of simple childlike faith. If only church doctrine remained so simple. Unfortunately, Christian beliefs grow in complexity like the equation $2 + 2 = 4$ progresses into algebra, geometry, and calculus.

Our love for Jesus compelled us to join a church where we came to understand what we recognize as faith. We hold to our unique interpretation of scripture and recognize how each of our churches has a different statement of that one faith. In the say way, "4" finds expression in an infinite number of equations like:

$$1 + 3 = 4 \qquad 10 - 6 = 4 \qquad \sqrt{16} = 4$$
$$96 \div 24 = 4 \qquad -2 \times -2 = 4 \qquad 2^2 = 4$$

These are only a few of the different ways we can express "4." Likewise, churches today have distinctive expressions of faith. Still, no church holds to the original simple statements of the first faith represented by the equation $2 + 2 = 4$.

Our various expressions of the one faith can be good. Some of these doctrines came about to correct abuses or errors throughout church history. Despite our many differences, we often comprehend

Our doctrines might be close to "4," but we have lost the original meaning of "2 + 2 = 4."

various doctrinal expressions of "4" made by other Christians like the equations above—they're just not our way to express "4."

However, sometimes the ways we express our doctrines are more than we can reconcile. We look at our unique creeds and statements of faith but struggle to agree on the meaning of "4." What they see as "4" doesn't add up because we see their different doctrines like:

$$1 + 2 \neq 4 \qquad 3 \times 2 \neq 4 \qquad 12 \div 2 \neq 4$$

$$27 - 3 \neq 4 \qquad -7(3x + 2y) \div (4a - b) \neq 4$$

Believers may comprehend the different doctrines held by others as something close to "4," but they don't recognize it as what their church teaches. At other times, Christians don't comprehend each other's faith equations and cannot agree with each other's stated beliefs. When this happens, an individual's idea of "4" views the "1 + 2" or "3 + 2" expressions of faith made by others as being far from the truth. The greater the perceived distance from "4" often causes Christians to break fellowship—some consider other believers heretics.

No matter how we might express "the faith" in our church, we believe in Jesus through our unique expression of "4." Our various equations of what we call "4" does not mean we do not have saving or trusting faith to receive Jesus as our LORD and Savior. The various ways Christians define "4" illustrates the differences between the creeds, doctrines, and teachings taught in our Churches as *"the faith."*

How can we come together from our various expressions of faith to contend together for *one faith*—the first faith described simply as $2 + 2 = 4$?

Contending for "the faith" begins as you, and I acknowledge the faith we ascribe to in our churches today is NOT the first faith. In so many ways, things were added to and subtracted from the first faith given by Jesus. Our doctrines might be close to "4," but we have lost the original meaning of "$2 + 2 = 4$."

Resurrected faith earnestly contends "for *the faith* that was once for all delivered to the saints." Unfortunately, the doctrines held by our churches may rely more upon the teaching and traditions of men as passed down to us than the *one faith first given.*

To recognize how what we believe drifted over time from "the faith" established and fulfilled by Jesus is a difficult pill to swallow. We struggle because our faith is precious to us. No one wants to admit they could be wrong, but it is the first step we must take.

From creation, God progressively revealed and perfectly fulfilled in Jesus *one faith,* not many. Today, the LORD calls for us to return to this singular faith made known in Christ.[10] With great care, we must be willing to examine the faith we individually hold as being true. Jesus said the Spirit "will guide you into all the truth" (John 16:13). With the help of the Holy Spirit, we can receive insight into how closely our faith aligns with the doctrine Jesus revealed, as illustrated by our various expressions of "4."

One LORD, One Faith

Our problem comes by putting the proverbial cart before the horse. We get things turned around and put our heads before our hearts when our pursuit of doctrinal truth comes before a heartfelt desire to know Jesus.

All our Bibles tell us the same thing: "There is *one LORD, one faith*" (Eph. 4:5, NLT emphasis mine). The "one LORD" is Jesus who makes known the "one faith." The order here is significant because an accumulation of doctrine does not mean you will know Jesus as He is. Doctrinal truth will teach you *about* Jesus but not give you a *revelation* of Jesus.

Knowledge about Jesus satisfies our dead faith religion. An accumulation of doctrine provides us with more information to increase one's head knowledge. Unfortunately, head knowledge alone is powerless to change our lives.

A revelation of Jesus animates resurrected faith with a passion that transforms our hearts. Knowing and loving Jesus overflows with a desire to please the LORD and not ourselves—a revelation of Jesus causes us to want to live just like Jesus.

Church history reveals, time and again, how a yearning for a revelation of Christ brings revival, while an emphasis on doctrines often leads to division. For better or worse, the people living in our neighborhoods who are not Christians are impacted by what happens within our churches. Revivals transform communities, but a divided church only further separates non-believers from Jesus.

The schisms and contradictions between Christian beliefs do not happen under the steeple behind closed doors. The lost in this world are watching us. They see our posts on social media. They read the doctrinal defenses for our beliefs and attacks against those who disagree with us.

People outside the Church often view Christians as narrow-minded and dismiss the gospel as outdated and not relevant for their lives today. While most non-Christians may say they believe in God or a divine being, they reject Jesus and our faith. Unfortunately, the fights they see between churches make them unable to distinguish between who Jesus is and our different doctrines about Him.

How have Christians, who represent Jesus before a fallen world and are called to make Him known, how have they failed in this all-important mission?

Many churches teach doctrine to make Jesus known rather than letting our knowledge of the person of Jesus define our doctrine. Each church and denomination present a different caricature of Jesus characterized by their statement of faith rather than the fullness of who He is. In one way or another, Christians know Jesus—they just know Him differently because of what their churches taught them.

In turn, many believers follow the example of their churches when talking with people about their faith. However, Jesus did not call us to win a debate. The LORD wants us to be a witness and tell the story of what He did and is doing in our lives.

Well-meaning Christians communicate head knowledge, trying to convince others to believe. Simply telling people about Jesus seldom leads to their salvation. Instead, believers should dialog with the hearts of non-believers to share their encounter with the risen Savior. The former opens the door to endless debate about doctrine

> *Now is the time to put first things first and allow the Holy Spirit to reveal Jesus because in knowing Him, we will all get a little closer to the one faith we each call "4."*

and who Jesus is. The latter introduces the person of Jesus, who stands ready to reveal Himself at an individual's point of need.

Pop culture accurately assesses the different doctrines and many Jesuses Christians worship. The TV program "American Gods" character Mr. Wednesday explains Jesus' multiple incarnations this way, "You've got your White, Jesuit-style Jesus, your Black African Jesus, your Mexican Jesus, and your swarthy Greek Jesus... There's a lot of need for Jesus, so there is a lot of Jesuses." Countless Jesuses make their cameo. Writer Bryan Fuller said, "There are so many different perspectives on who Jesus Christ was and is in the hearts of those who worship him, so that I think it's interesting to say to Christians that your Jesus—[pointing]—is different from your Jesus."[11]

You and I probably find the idea of more than one Jesus offensive. However, a smack in the face like this might be just what we need to awaken us to how our churches uniquely recreated Jesus according to their doctrinal image.

Our LORD Jesus Christ does not suffer from an identity crisis! He is the one true God, the eternal, self-existent "I AM" (Exod. 3:14;

John 8:58). Intellectually we affirm this truth, but we struggle to understand the depth of meaning and know the "I AM" accurately.

Sir Isaac Newton said, "What we know is a drop; what we don't know is an ocean."[12] What you and I claim to know about God is only a drop compared to the vast waters of God's identity. Will we stop following our heads into an accumulation of more and more doctrine about Jesus and, instead, allow our hearts to venture into the limitless depths of who God is with a passion for knowing Jesus more fully?

Jesus wants to make Himself known, saying to His disciples the Holy Spirit "will bear witness about me" and "will guide you into all the truth" (John 15:26; 16:13). The Spirit will help us let go of teaching added to the first faith and receive things subtracted from it the more we know Jesus. Now is the time for us to allow the Holy Spirit to open our spiritual eyes and give us fresh insight to know Jesus as He is.

The Church needs to be reminded there is only one Jesus, not many. We have *one LORD* who reveals *one faith*.

"Just as it is useless for a farmer to continue sowing if the weeds have not been pulled, so it is fruitless to announce the truth if the lie is not confronted."[13] The Church unknowingly created many Jesuses with its many doctrines. Jude wants us to contend for *"the faith,"* resurrected faith that is authentic and alive because it springs forth from the person of Jesus.

For you "to contend for the faith" means holding what you believe in an open hand. You think you comprehend what faith is, like "2 + 2 = 4." Only God's Spirit can help you recognize what was added to or subtracted from the first faith within the doctrines you believe.

Don't make the mistake of thinking *a faith* in God or Jesus is good enough. Dead faith doctrine will never do. You need a singular resurrected faith that stands above all others because it alone is true.

Now is the time to put first things first and allow the Holy Spirit to reveal Jesus because in knowing Him, we will all get a little closer to the *one faith* we each call "4."

Contending for Resurrected Faith

✝ We take a stand to contend as combatants against anything in opposition to our common salvation, the living faith Jesus gave once and for all to the saints.

   o We refuse to yield to cultural relativism but recognize that truth is absolute.

   o We resist the doctrines and traditions of man within the church that are contrary to the first faith.

✝ The heart of a contender recognizes the distinctive difference between believing faith and "the faith" we contend for.

   o Believing faith, defined as one's confidence or trust in God, is impacted by circumstances.

   o Believing faith waxes and wanes from a sure hope capable of moving mountains to a skeptical question overcome by anxiety and doubts.

   o "The faith" is an unshakable foundation of doctrinal truth progressively revealed by God since creation and perfectly fulfilled in the person of Jesus.

✝ Resurrected faith originates from a wholehearted desire to intimately know Jesus through the personal experience of His life, love, and presence and not one's religious activity.

✝ We contend for one faith, which is singular and complete in Christ because "the faith" is not one among many Christian beliefs or doctrines.

- o Just as different mathematical equations can state the idea of "4," we respect the distinctive expressions of doctrine made by other followers of Jesus.

- o We "contend for the faith" with an awareness that none of our churches accurately convey the first faith represented by the simple equation "$2 + 2 = 4$."

✝ We have one LORD Jesus Christ who reveals in Himself one faith.

- o Non-believers see the doctrinal disagreements between churches creating caricatures formed by our different doctrines to portray many Jesuses.

- o Jesus commissioned Christians to be witnesses telling the story of what He did and is doing in their lives, not trying to convince non-believers through debate.

Notes: Chapter 4 "Contenders of the Faith"

[1] Preaching Today. "Churchill's Real 'Never Give Up' Speech." Accessed February 16, 2018. http://www.preachingtoday.com/illustrations/2003/january/14 163.html

[2] Dictionary.com. "Contend" Accessed February 16, 2018. http://www.dictionary. com/browse/contend

[3] The Greek word *epagōnizomai* is a compound word joining *epi,* a preposition that strengthens the root of the word *agōnizomai* translated "contend." Lexicon :: Strong's G1864 - Epagōnizomai n.d. BlueLetterBible.org. See Vine's Expository Dictionary. Accessed February 16, 2018. https://www.blueletterbible.org/lang/lexicon/lexicon.cfm?Strongs=G1864&t=ESV

[4] The etymology of the English word agony comes from the Greek word *agōnizomai* translated "strive" or "fight." Lexicon :: Strong's G75 - Agōnizomai n.d. BlueLetterBible.org. Accessed February 16, 2018. https://www.blueletterbible.org/lang/lexicon/lexicon.cfm?Strongs=G75&t=ESV

[5] Holmes, Arthur F. *The Idea of a Christian College.* Grand Rapids, MI.: Wm. B. Eerdmans Publishing Co., 1987. p. 7.

[6] See Matthew 8:10; Romans 14:1.

[7] See Matthew 8:23-26; 17:19-20.

[8] See John 15:26.

[9] Webster, Allen "Why Do Churches of Christ Not Use Instrumental Music." HouseToHouse.com. Accessed March 1, 2020. https://housetohouse.com/why-do-churches-of-christ-not-use-instrumental-music/

[10] See Colossians 1:15-20

[11] Griffiths, Eleanor Bley. "American Gods mythology guide: Meet Mexican Jesus, White Jesus and Black Jesus." (June 2, 2017), RadioTimes.com Accessed March 2, 2020. https://www.radiotimes.com/news/2017-06-02/american-gods-mythology-guide -meet-mexican-white-jesus-and-black-jesus/

[12] Isaac Newton Quotes. GoodReads.com. Accessed March 14, 2018. https://www.goodreads.com/author/quotes/135106.Isaac_Newton

[13] Harris, Ralph W. (General Editor). *The New Testament Study Bible: Hebrews - Jude.* Springfield, MO: The Complete Biblical Library, 1989. p. 528.

Chapter 5

Don't Be Fooled

*Those who consider themselves religious and yet
do not keep a tight rein on their tongues deceive
themselves, and their religion is worthless.*

James 1:26 (NIV)

In the summer of 1943, the Nazis tightened their grip on Europe with the Atlantic Wall, a 1,500-mile coastal fortification. At the same time, the Allies planned an invasion at Normandy, the epicenter of an attack to liberate the continent from German occupation. The key to success was more than a battle plan. A year of planning and preparation also included an elaborate deception designed to fool Hitler and the German High Command.

The disinformation campaign, codenamed Operation Bodyguard, worked. As Allied forces landed in Normandy on D-Day, June 6, 1944, Hitler believed the attack there was a ruse. The Nazis were convinced an imminent invasion would be made at Pas de Calis in France, the shortest distance across the English Channel from Great Britain. One hundred fifty miles northeast of Normandy, much-needed reinforcements waited at Calis to defend against Allied invaders who never came. Hitler was fooled.[1]

Don't let Satan fool you! The enemy is the master of deception, "the father of lies" (John 8:44). The devil wants to pull the wool over your eyes. All too often, he succeeds with a double agent you never suspect.

You and I are our own worst enemies. We lie to ourselves more than anyone else, more than to our spouses, children, extended family, and friends combined. Every day we tell ourselves everything is okay and ignore the still small voice calling us to Jesus.

Dead faith creates a deadly deception to keep us from coming to Jesus for a faith resurrection.

Across the centuries, Jude urges us not to believe the lie but "to contend for the faith" and struggle daily to know Jesus more fully. Consider his plea once more. A rough literal English translation of the word order used by Jude says, "[to contend earnestly] [for the] [once for all] [having been delivered] [to the] [saints] [faith].[2] Here, the seven brackets represent the seven Greek words that account for fourteen or more words when translated into our English Bibles.

In the previous chapter, we looked at the beginning and end of Jude's appeal for us [to contend earnestly] [for the] [faith]. This plea is the heart cry of his urgent message. However, his words in the center, [once for all] [having been delivered] [to the] [saints], focus our understanding. So, let's take aim to comprehend our struggle for the faith more fully.

Once For All Time

We fight to know Jesus and the first faith He gave "once for all." The Greek word Jude used describes something *completed to establish perpetual validity with no need for repetition.*[3] In Christ, "the faith" is settled and fixed for all time because it is grounded in Jesus' identity as LORD and what He accomplished for us.

"Once for all" indicates the completion of God's progressive self-revelation and the first faith. From creation, the LORD began to make known His identity. God's divine download was slow and gradual, like watching an artist begin to put paint on a canvas. Only the artist's imagination could see how the colors would blend and come together to create a masterpiece.

The brushstrokes of God's self-disclosure began with Adam and Eve, but His self-portrait was far from complete. Throughout the chapters of Old Testament history, God continued to put paint to the canvas of human hearts with ever-increasing awe and wonder. Little by little, the masterpiece of the knowledge of the LORD continued to grow in man's understanding. Finally, God revealed the ultimate fullness of His nature and being in Jesus.

The writer of Hebrews recognized the various ways and many times God revealed Himself to their ancestors through the prophets. Then, at long last, the time came when God spoke "to us by His Son, whom He appointed heir of all things, and through whom also He made the universe. The Son is the radiance of God's glory *and the exact representation of His being*" (Heb. 1:1-3, NIV emphasis mine).

Jesus did not say, "It is to be added to or subtracted from" because He perfectly finished all the work given to Him by the Father.

Everything changed with Jesus because the LORD communicated personally to His people in Him. Little by little, God's revelation of Himself grew through the parts and portions within the Old Testament. But, at just the right time, God's self-disclosure culminated with crystal clarity through His "perfect, absolute, final revelation in God the Son."[4] Jesus left nothing out—to know Jesus is to comprehend the LORD'S identity as He is.

Jesus said, "I and the Father are one," and He is the "exact representation" of God, "who does not change like shifting shadows" (John 10:30; James 1:17, NIV). The identity of Jesus and what He did define our doctrine because to know Jesus is to know God as He truly is.

Jesus said, "My words will never pass away," so the first faith He established endures unchanged for all time (Matt. 24:35; Mark 13:31; Luke 21:33). Christ revealed "once for all" what we can believe and know about God with eternal effectiveness and no need for repetition.

Jesus breathed His last saying, "It is finished" (John 19:30). Our LORD'S final words from the cross brought God's plan of redemption to its culmination *and* completed His revelation of God to man. Jesus did not say, "It is to be added to or subtracted from" because He perfectly finished *all* the work given to Him by the Father.

While God's identity and the first faith are revealed in Christ "once for all," we should not make a mistake and think we know the LORD in all His fullness. How can the finite mind of man grasp the infinite nature of who God is in His fullness?

Until Jesus comes again, we strive to know Him just as He entirely knows us "for now we see in a mirror dimly, but then face to face" (1 Cor. 13:12). Our limited vision is why we must "contend for the faith" to know Christ more and more.

Obtained Faith

Our charge is "to contend for the faith that was once for all delivered." The word translated "delivered" means to convey or communicate verbally.[5] The LORD spoke the first faith as His self-revelation of God to man. No one invented what we believe by writing it down because "delivered" means God handed down to man what we believe—God revealed "the faith" to make it knowable.[6]

Paul bears witness to this saying, "The gospel that was preached by me is not man's gospel. For I did not receive it from any man, nor was I taught it..." He did not sit in a classroom for instruction, nor did he invent doctrines of the Christian faith. Instead, Paul said, *"I received it through a revelation of Jesus Christ"* (Gal. 1:11-12, emphasis mine). Paul's testimony is clear—he first came to know the LORD Jesus and then, in turn, to understand the first faith in its fullness.

Think for a moment about who Paul was before he came to know Jesus as Messiah and LORD. Previously known as Saul, he grew up in "the faith" given by God as the Jews then understood it. Saul "studied under Gamaliel" and was "a Hebrew of Hebrews; in regard to the law, a Pharisee" (Acts 22:3; Phil.3:5, NIV).

Saul's zeal for the LORD was so great he persecuted followers of the Way by arresting and putting them to death. He received letters of authority to go to Damascus to find any believers living there and bring them back to Jerusalem to stand trial. He wanted to bring an end to what he and other God-fearing Jews considered a distortion of the true faith the LORD entrusted to them.[7]

But on the road to Damascus, Saul had a revelation of Jesus that changed everything. As a Pharisee, he thought he knew the LORD through his years of study. But then, unexpectedly, the Old Testament scriptures came to life to reveal Jesus. At that moment, God aligned Saul's thinking with the first faith established at creation and perfectly fulfilled by Jesus. "A revelation of Jesus" brought clarity to a lifetime of learning to see the LORD where Saul had not seen Him before.

Saul no longer understood God and the Scriptures through the misinterpreted doctrines and traditions handed down to first century Jews. Instead, with resurrected faith, he recognized the identity of the LORD or *Yahweh* in Jesus Christ. This revelation brought about an immediate transformation. Saul began to preach the gospel he set out to silence, "and confounded the Jews who lived in Damascus by proving that Jesus was the Christ." (Acts 9:22).

Named after Israel's first king, Saul even changed his name to Paul, meaning small or little.[8] The Holy Spirit transformed Paul's years of religious head knowledge to give him a heartfelt desire to make Jesus Christ and not himself known.

Paul's testimony teaches us two valuable lessons. First, with "a revelation of Jesus," the Holy Spirit makes dead faith come alive. And second, "a revelation of Jesus" corrects the twisted views and distorted doctrines people believe about God. Resurrected faith awakens us to know the LORD Jesus and the faith He reveals more fully.

From the beginning, God revealed His identity and the first faith. But unfortunately, over time, misguided teaching and traditions of the Jews distorted it. By the first century, Jewish teachers of the law added to and subtracted from the first faith to create seven different Jewish sects, each with their unique doctrines.

With roots in the intertestamental period, these seven branches of Judaism impacted the culture in the days of Jesus and the Early Church—Pharisees, Sadducees, Essenes, Herodians, Scribes, Zealots, and Samaritans.[9] Their distortion of the faith is why many Jews, like Paul, did not recognize Jesus as the LORD when He came.

Jesus told the religious teachers, "You search the Scriptures because you think that in them you have eternal life; and it is they that *bear witness about me*, yet you refuse to come to me that you may have life" (John 5:39-40, emphasis mine). Jesus went on to say that Moses would testify against them because "if you believed Moses, you would believe me; for he wrote of me" (verse 46).

From generation to generation, the doctrines and traditions of the Jewish people departed from the first faith given by God through Moses and the other prophets. As a result, they could not see Jesus for who He was nor accept His teaching. Their various man-made doctrines and traditions blinded them. Many, like Paul, were zealous for their faith but failed to hold steadfast and "contend for the faith" God made known to them through the Scriptures.

As it was then, so it is for you and me today. Resurrected faith is only obtained from heaven as "a revelation of Jesus Christ."

The Holy Spirit wants to do the same work in us. The Spirit's call "to contend for the faith" is not a work to replace Christian doctrines in itself, but to remedy the error of our ways and enlighten our understanding of who Jesus is. Our faith needs a correction and not cancelation—to restore things taken away and remove teaching added to "the faith" first given.

Jude urged first century believers to struggle for "the faith that was once for all delivered." In Christ, God delivered and spoke His word because Jesus is the Word incarnate.[10] By His Word, the LORD entrusted His identity and the faith to all who would believe. Jesus came to make God known. The living Word revealed Himself to them to clarify the first faith.

In the same way, "the faith" has been given to us by "a revelation of Jesus Christ" because "faith comes from hearing, and hearing through the word of Christ" (Rom. 10:17).

The teachings of Jesus, Paul, Peter, or other Apostles and New Testament authors did not invent what we call the Christian doctrine. Christian faith, the first faith, is older than the writing of the New Testament. Everything God previously revealed in the Old Testament, from creation to the cross, all culminated in the person of Jesus.

Look again upon Jesus' face. Like Paul and the saints who have gone before us, the Holy Spirit will set our hearts ablaze to know Jesus and the first faith He reveals.

We obtain and contend for resurrected faith only through "a revelation of Jesus Christ" to know Him as He truly is.

We must be careful not to make the same mistake as first century Jews and fail to recognize Jesus because we hold onto our various doctrines and traditions. We, too, can become just as dogmatic and Pharisaical about what our churches teach today. Our different dead faith beliefs define the LORD rather than "a revelation of Jesus" defining our doctrine.

Some people mistakenly believe Jesus taught a new faith to establish the Christian Church. However, the purpose of Jesus' teaching and the rest of the New Testament was not to do away with the teaching of the Old Testament or Jewish faith per se. Instead, His goal was to correct their distorted and misaligned view and restore the first faith they lost over time.

As He did then, Jesus wants to resurrect our dead faith religion with a living faith. Jesus came to make God known to man. He did this so dead faith might be revived and realigned with the bedrock of truth, the first faith, progressively declared from creation with its final culmination perfectly revealed in Jesus Himself.

We obtain and contend for resurrected faith only through "a revelation of Jesus Christ" to know Him as He truly is.

Obligation of the Saints

Jude says the first faith was once for all time handed down "to the saints." Like most Christians today, you probably don't think of yourself as a saint, but God does. You are a saint not because of what you do but simply by your faith in Jesus. The Greek word translated as "saints" describes us as a holy people who have been "set apart for God to be, as it were, exclusively His."[11] We are consecrated for God's purpose and not our self-centered desires.

Resurrected faith understands far greater joy is ours when we join the struggle to know "the faith" through a revelation of Jesus than follow our desire for self-gratification.

As saints, Jesus entrusted us as guardians of "the faith." You and I received a divine purpose and God-given obligation. All believers are given this responsibility and not just supposed "super-saints" we call pastors. God set us apart to contend earnestly and protect "the faith" handed down from generation to generation.

We need a strategy to fulfill our obligation as saints to "the faith." Paul likewise instructs followers of Jesus to "fight the good fight of faith... guard what God has trusted to you." (1 Tim. 6:12, 20, NCV).

The context in First Timothy chapter six provides four steps we must take to fulfill our responsibility as guardians of "the faith." I've stated these as four E's. As saints, our fourfold obligation to the faith calls us to examine, engender, expose, and exemplify.

Examine Our Faith to Prove it is Genuine

The first step is vital—you and I must test ourselves to see that we are in "the faith." Don't be afraid to examine your beliefs because if your faith is genuine, it can and will stand up to any test. On the other hand, if what you believe is not sound doctrine, it must be unmasked. Never forget, we must fight not to be deceived by what we consider trustworthy but is false doctrine.[12]

Paul provides a simple test of our faith. A false or different doctrine "does not agree with the sound words of our LORD Jesus Christ and the teaching that accords with godliness" (1 Tim. 6:3). Therefore, anything we believe that contradicts the words of Jesus or biblical instruction in righteousness is not aligned with the first faith.

You and I cannot examine our faith in isolation. Steve Walent, a missionary to Germany, said, "The Early Church and Christians today outside the influence of Western Culture instinctively understand they are members of a community. However, American Christians and others in the West, like Europe, tend to focus instead on the individual."[13]

If we are not careful, our western emphasis on personal faith will fool us into thinking we can make it on our own. Rather than continue to isolate yourself from other believers, choose to swim upstream counter to the cultural mindset around us. Individual believers are one body in Christ, so "each one of us is joined with one another, *and we become together what we could not be alone.*" (Rom. 12:5, VOICE).

We need accountable relationships with other believers to pass the test—we can't do it by ourselves. Without the help of the Holy Spirit and other believers, we are blind to the smallest sins in our lives. The mistaken belief we are in the faith because we don't struggle with so-called "BIG SINS" demonstrates our lack of discernment and knowledge of the truth.

Dead faith is blind faith, unaware of how much we need each other to pass the test. Only together can we see whether or not we are in the faith by what we say and do—how we live our lives from day to day according to the truth of God's Word. Living faith recognizes our need and responsibility to examine our faith within an accountable community of believers. Allow others to put your faith to the test with questions like these:

- How have you twisted Jesus' words to fit your beliefs?
- How does the teaching of Jesus make you uncomfortable?
- What changes do you need to make so your beliefs align with Jesus' teaching?
- Does what you believe only apply to you and others like you, or are your beliefs true for everyone everywhere?
- How does your faith impact the way you daily live your life?
- Does your behavior align with the teaching about godliness?
- How will biblical instruction in righteousness change what you do and say?

Resurrected faith will pass the test of faith through obedience to the words of Jesus and biblical instruction in righteousness. Only then will the activity of *"faithing"* enable us to live more and more like our LORD.

Engender the Life of Faith in Others

As saints, the second step to fulfill our obligation is to reproduce living faith in the lives of new believers. Paul reminded Timothy to "take hold of the eternal life to which you were called and about which you made the good confession in the presence of many witnesses" (1 Tim. 6:12). We must share "the good confession" and testimony of faith with others.

The natural reproduction of life occurs within nature with little or no effort. From creation, God ordained every living thing would reproduce "according to its kind" (Gen. 1:11,12,21,25). The great variety of plants and animals all share one thing in common. Each produces offspring just like itself.

What is true in the natural world is true spiritually as well. Christ-followers should reproduce other Christ-followers—disciples make other disciples. We see this pattern in the book of Acts. Believers who received the first faith were actively sharing it with others so that "the LORD added to their number day by day those who were being saved." (Acts 2:47).

In the first century, resurrected faith gave birth to believers overflowing with reproductive energy. The same should be true today. You and I should engender the life of Jesus within the lives of people around us.

Children automatically share the DNA of their parents. Spiritual DNA follows the same pattern. Jesus imparted the DNA of living faith to His followers, and they passed that DNA on to the next generation of believers and so on. Believers in the first century did not rely upon special programs to see people saved. Instead, the Holy Spirit empowered them to be Jesus' witnesses, naturally reproducing living faith with the life of Jesus in others.

Today, the unfortunate reality is that much of American Christianity produces little more than sterile church attenders incapable of reproducing the life of Jesus in others. Sadly, our spiritual DNA has been altered.

We have made the process of spiritual reproduction to eternal life more complicated than it really is. What should happen naturally now takes more effort because men's religious precepts and traditions were added to and subtracted from the first faith. We tend to debate doctrines to convince people to believe, but the Holy Spirit does not empower us to become spiritual defense attorneys for Jesus. Instead, the Spirit energizes us as witnesses to simply tell others the story of what the life of Jesus does within our lives.

Our faith needs to undergo spiritual genetic testing to determine how our DNA was corrupted from the original DNA of Jesus. The first faith with the DNA of Jesus is alive and vibrant with the power of eternal life.

We should see the reproduction of life in others through the spiritual DNA of Jesus within us. Like those in the Early Church, we should boldly share our faith with others wherever we are—places like our homes, schools, and workplaces. As parents, we should instruct our children in "the faith," so it is alive in them and reproduced in their generation. As students or employees, we should not be ashamed of the gospel in our schools or workplaces but share the life we have received.

Resurrected faith is reproduced bountifully to draw those still dead in their sins to saving faith in Jesus as their LORD and savior. Our desire is to contend for and share a living faith grounded in the knowledge of who Jesus truly is.

God wants to resurrect our dead faith, so faith with the DNA of Jesus is again naturally reproduced in the lives of new believers.

Expose the Lie of Counterfeit Faith

The third step we must take as guardians is the obligation to unmask counterfeit faith and expose what is contrary to the truth. Paul identified those who taught a fraudulent doctrine as boastful people without understanding. He told Timothy they craved controversy, were quick to argue, caused envy and division, belittled others with slander, questioned authority, continued to stir up trouble, and were warped in their thinking.

Paul further showed how false teachers taught things contrary to sound doctrine because they were "depraved in mind and deprived of the truth, imagining that godliness is a means of gain" (1 Tim. 6:5). He continued exposing how their passion for money and the things it can buy leads them into all kinds of evil. Unfortunately, their bad example and deceptive teaching were contagious, causing some to wander "away from the faith" (verse 10). Others with tongue-in-cheek religious talk and "contradictions of what is falsely called 'knowledge'... swerved from the faith" (verses 20-21).

We must remain vigilant in our stand today against what Paul called "a different doctrine" because it is seductive (verse 3). While tantalizing teachings have no real value, deceptive doctrines appeal to our desires with the illusion of truth and satisfaction. Sadly, counterfeit faith leaves those fooled bankrupt and far from the genuine.

People who handle currency regularly receive training to recognize counterfeit money. "Each note includes security and design features unique to how the denomination is used in circulation."[14] Bank tellers, cashiers, and others are taught to recognize these features on legal currency and expose the counterfeit. They do this not by studying the counterfeit but by constantly handling genuine real money.

While not called to a witch hunt, we must be prepared to unmask the counterfeit faith and expose it as false. We do not need to study cults or fraudulent beliefs. Instead, our focus is twofold. First, we need a growing passion for an intimate knowledge of Jesus because to know Him is to comprehend the first faith. Second, we must continually examine our beliefs to pass the test and not wander into error.

Should we fail to expose the counterfeit, then not only do we risk being deceived, but others, too, might embrace doctrines with no value as though they were priceless. Jesus is "the truth" (John 14:6). The more we come to know Him and make Him known, the better prepared we and others will be to recognize faith that is not authentic.

In book three, *Resurrected Faith: Winning the Battle for Living Faith,* we will look more deeply at how to expose those Jude identified as "ungodly people, who pervert the grace of our God" (Jude 1:4). Again, our love for Jesus should compel us to unmask masquerading wolves disguised as harmless sheep.

Exemplify the Faith Every Day

As saints, our fourth step requires us to exemplify "the faith" in our daily lives. Paul did not want Timothy to wander aimlessly but demonstrate his faith was alive as an example for others to follow. How Timothy lived his life from day to day mattered.

Paul's charge to Timothy applies equally to us today. As men and women of God, we need to "flee these things," running from anything produced by a counterfeit faith in steadfast pursuit of "righteousness, godliness, faith, love, steadfastness, [and] gentleness" (verse 11). Like Timothy, we are to obey our LORD's command and live our lives "unstained and free from reproach until the appearing of our LORD Jesus Christ" (verse 14).

Resurrected faith will be evident in how we live—an example for others to follow. We cannot merely profess sound doctrine or claim to believe in Christ. We are to embody a life of faith in how we think, speak, and act.

The fool remains content to just believe. Contenders realize living faith energizes them to live what they believe.

As Christ-followers, we are "to live up to the life to which God called you" (Eph. 4:1, NCV). The Greek word translated "live up to" or in the NIV, "live a life" literally means "walk."[15] Every step we take on the path of life determines our behavior at any given moment and our lifestyle, so we need to be careful how we walk.

Don't be fooled because how we walk from day to day reveals the depth of our love for Jesus. You and I cannot hide the evidence of our intimate knowledge of Jesus any more than I can hide my love for Susie. The love for *"My Bride,"* as I call her, is evident every day in what I say and do. In the same way, we daily express our love for Jesus through everything we say and do. Our LORD'S words and the whisper of His Spirit bring our faith to life and empower us to live what we believe.

Perhaps you remember the "WWJD" fad. Christians wore these letters on T-shirts, wristbands, and more to remember to ask themselves, "What Would Jesus Do?" That's the wrong question. Instead, believers should ask themselves, "WIJD—*What IS Jesus Doing.*" The resurrected Christ is still active today. By the power of the Holy Spirit, Jesus wants to transform our lives to align with His. Jesus will make a radical transformation in every aspect of how we live our lives—a change others cannot help but notice.

Just like children learn to imitate their parents, so too, resurrected faith emulates the life of Jesus. Living faith recognizes what Jesus is doing today in and through our lives, so we live differently—we imitate our LORD. The words that cross our lips agree with what Jesus says. Our actions line up with how Jesus lived.

Resurrected faith loves and listens to Jesus, so the way we "walk" each day is forever changed. Anything less is hypocrisy.

The Choice

Jude's ancient call confronts us with a choice. We can choose to play the fool sitting on the sidelines disengaged, or we can determine to engage in the struggle for what we believe as a contender. The choice is ours.

Contenders recognize "the faith" endures unchanged, given once for all time. They know faith was obtained, not through the study of doctrine but by a revelation of Jesus. Once received, contenders accept their obligation as saints set apart for God's purpose to examine, engender, expose, and exemplify genuine faith.

The fool remains content to just believe. Contenders realize living faith energizes them to live what they believe. While the fool continues in a spiritual slumber, contenders hear the Spirit's call to wake up to the dangers of dead faith.

Don't be deceived. Resurrected faith fuels a passion "to contend for the faith that was once for all delivered to the saints."

Contending for Resurrected Faith

✟ A master of deception, the devil wants to fool us, so we mistakenly think joining the battle "to contend for the faith" is unnecessary.

✟ We contend for resurrected faith given once and for all time through an intimate knowledge of Jesus Christ.

- o "Once for all" establishes "the faith" as a never-ending reality, fixed forever in the identity of Jesus.

- o "Once for all" shows the completion of God's progressive revelation of Himself, beginning at creation with its perfect and complete fulfillment in Jesus.

✟ We contend for resurrected faith "that was once for all delivered."

- o "Delivered" means "the faith" was obtained or handed down from God as the LORD spoke to make faith known.

- o "The faith" was not the invention of any man but is received "through a revelation of Jesus Christ."

- o "A revelation of Jesus Christ" brings dead faith to life, correcting people's twisted beliefs about God.

✟ As saints, we are set apart with a divine obligation to:

- o Examine our faith with the help of other believers to prove it is genuine.

- o Engender "the faith," reproducing the life-giving DNA of Jesus in others.

- ○ Expose the lie of counterfeit faith, so deceitful doctrines are not accepted as genuine, and
- ○ Exemplify a life of faith to live what we believe, imitating Jesus in what we say and do.

Notes: Chapter 5 "Don't Be Fooled"

[1] "Fooling Hitler: The Elaborate Ruse Behind D-Day." History.com. (August 30, 2018), Accessed May 7, 2021. https://www.history.com/news/fooling-hitler-the-elaborate-ruse-behind-d-day

[2] Jude 1:3 English Standar Version (ESV) Interlinear BlueLetterBible.org. Accessed March 21, 2018. https://www.blueletterbible.org/esv/jde/1/3/p0/t_concf_1167003

[3] The Greek word hapax translated "once for all" (emphasis mine). Lexicon:: Strongs G530 - Hapax n.d. BlueLetterBible.org. Accessed March 13, 2020. https://www.blueletterbible.org/lang/lexicon/lexicon.cfm?Strongs=G530&t=ESV

[4] Lloyd-Jones, D. Martyn. *Authority*. Carlisle, PA. Banner of Truth, 1984. p. 60.

[5] Delivered is the translation of the Greek word *paradidōmi*. Lexicon :: Strong's G3860 - *Paradidōmi*. n.d. BlueLetterBible.org. See Thayer's Greek Lexicon. Accessed March 18, 2020. https://www.blueletterbible.org/lang/lexicon/lexicon.cfm?Strongs=G3860&t=ESV

[6] The Greek word *paradidōmi* was written in the passive voice, which means God and not man was active. Jude 1:3 English Standar Version (ESV) Interlinear.

[7] See Acts 22:4-5; Romans 2:3.

[8] Lexicon :: Strong's G3972 - Paulos n.d. BlueLetterBible.org. See outline of Biblical Usage. Accessed July 15, 2020. https://www.blueletterbible.org/lang/lexicon/lexicon.cfmStrongs=G3972&t=ESV

[9] Jacoby, Douglas. "The Spectrum of Judaism in the 1st Century AD." (July 13, 2013) DouglasJacoby.com Accessed October 21, 2019. https://www.douglasjacoby.com/the-spectrum-of-judaism-in-the-1st-century-ad/

[10] See John 1:1.

[11] The Greek word *hagios* is often translated "saints" and literally means "set apart." Lexicon :: Strong's G40 – *hagios* n.d. BlueLetterBible.org. See Thayer's Greek Lexicon. Accessed December 18, 2018. https://www.blueletterbible.org/lang/lexicon/lexicon.cfm?Strongs=G40&t=ESV

[12] See James 1:22-27.

[13] Walent, Steve. Interview. June 19, 2020

[14] "The Seven Denominations." USCurrency.gov. Accessed March 29, 2018. https://www.uscurrency.gov/denominations

[15] The Greek word *peripateō* is translated literally as "walk" in the KJV, NKJV, ASV, ESV and NASB, other modern English translations interpret it as how we live. Lexicon :: Strong's G4043 – *Peripateō* n.d. BlueLetterBible.org. Accessed March 29, 2019. https://www.blueletterbible.org/lang/lexicon/lexicon.cfm?Strongs=G4043&t=ESV

Chapter 6

The Contender's Identity

I pray that your hearts will be flooded with light
so that you can understand the confident hope He
has given to those He called—His holy people.

Ephesians 1:18 (NLT)

A theme in Shakespeare's "Hamlet" is uncertainty—what many today might call an identity crisis. Ophelia voices this idea when she says, "We know what we are, but not what we may be." Both Hamlet and Ophelia are distressed by who they are and apprehensive about their future selves. Their identity crisis drove Ophelia to take her life in madness and Hamlet to put off his desire for revenge—a delay that cost him his life.[1]

In one way or another, we all go through an identity crisis.

Teachers do not instruct students about the social hierarchy in school. Instead, kids learn from each other the pecking order of who fits in and who does not. Everybody wants to be somebody, but not everyone makes the grade. Kids try to elevate their status and outdo each other in many different ways—some succeed and rise to the top of the class, while others fail.

I remember a time in high school when I felt an inner uncertainty about who I was. Like other days, I sat in the cafeteria with my four friends. Another group of our classmates made an outburst that overcame the usual cafeteria buzz. Suddenly, everyone seemed to be cheering and laughing, except my friends and others sitting nearby. An eerie realization hit me. I thought to myself, *"We're all nobodies. What will it take for them to include me?"* The look in my friends' eyes seemed to ask the same question, but, like me, they too were clueless about how to become somebody special.

Trying To Be Somebody

The desire to achieve and be extraordinary affects how we approach to God. Our attitude is a lot like Jesus' disciples. They each wanted to be the greatest. Jesus told them plainly, "If anyone would be first, he must be last of all and servant of all" (Mark 9:35). To drive the point home, Jesus picked up a child and said, "Whoever receives one such child in my name receives me" (verse 37).

You think that would be enough to change their way of thinking. It wasn't.

Within days people brought their children to Jesus for His blessing, but "the disciples rebuked them" (Mark 10:13). How quickly they forgot Jesus' object lesson. By turning the children away, the disciples alienated themselves from Jesus. They made judgments by the standards of the world and thought Jesus had more important things to do than spend time with children.

When Jesus saw what was going on, He was grieved. Forcefully He said, "Let the children come to me; do not hinder

Dead faith feelings of inferiority or superiority always keep us far from closeness to Jesus.

them." Rather than please Jesus, their best intentions irritated Him. Jesus continued, *"to such belongs the kingdom of God.* Truly, I say to you, whoever does not receive the kingdom of God like a child shall not enter it" (Mark 10:14-15, emphasis mine). Not only did the disciples' actions not welcome Jesus, but their critical attitudes also showed how God would likewise turn them away unless their hearts were changed.

We are sometimes just like Jesus' disciples.

I regret how I looked down upon some childlike adults attending our church. They were loud and sometimes did things to embarrass me. My dead faith judgment thought they were only looking for handouts. I'm grateful the LORD was patient with me and used them to teach me what childlike faith should look like in my life.

At one time or another, all of us thought more highly of ourselves than we should, holding similar unwise evaluations. James echoed the LORD'S rebuke to believers with dead faith religion, saying, "if you show favoritism, *you sin*" (James 2:9, NIV, emphasis mine). Our thoughts toward others are not harmless private opinions. Instead, Jesus sees our negative attitudes toward others as alienating hurtful perceptions that are, in a word, sin.

In much the same way, some people judge themselves unfairly. Looking down upon themselves, the enemy works to make them feel unworthy of entering the LORD'S presence. Therefore, they think they need to clean up their act, change some bad habits, or just be a better person for God to accept them.

The list of reasons people shared with me for not going to church usually focuses on one of these two extremes to be somebody. Either, they believe the lie that they are not good enough to come to God but desperately need some self-improvement. Or, like the disciples, they think too highly of themselves and want to be the greatest—they blindly imagine they are better than everyone else.

Dead faith feelings of inferiority or superiority always keep us far from closeness to Jesus.

"Just as I Am" But Not Alone

One's welcome into Jesus' presence or merit in His eyes is not based upon performance or status. We are not accepted because we wash off our sins. Nor do we deserve His acceptance because we are better than other people. None of those things matter.

The trusting faith of a child is all we need to approach the LORD. We must learn God loves us for who we are and not for anything we can do. Remember, Jesus taught His disciples that childlike faith is the key to inheriting the kingdom of God. Jesus is not looking for spiritual superstars or squeaky-clean saints.

The LORD wants us to come openly and honestly without pretense or spiritual charade. No need to try to be someone we are not. We try in vain to earn the right to enter Jesus' presence because it is impossible to impress God. Everyone must be real and come to Jesus like the old song says, "just as I am."

Driving a school bus full of elementary students, I saw firsthand how kids strive to be seen as someone important. Their effort to fit in and find their place in the crowd over a school year is amazing. Dr. Seuss understood the need for children to accept themselves as exceptional individuals when he wrote, *"Today you are You, that is truer than true. There is no one alive who is Youer than You."*[2]

The first step to being "You" is to be true to yourself and stop pretending to be something or someone you are not.

Jesus' disciples were looking out for number one—they put their best face on in a competition against each other to build up their egos and be recognized as the greatest. They are not alone.

A similar identity clash developed among those to whom Jude wrote. False teachers snuck into the church because so many were playing charades with their identity—they were not authentic to themselves, nor each other. With little or no accountability, they only concerned themselves with their personal faith and what seemed right in their own eyes.

Today, we make the same mistake as those Jude wrote to so long ago. Like children on a school bus, we try to impress others and maintain the appearance of being faithful Christians. We resist authenticity and accountability. As a result, our relationships with other believers are superficial, not significant. Jude did not urge us to

Resurrected faith recognizes our need for each other.

fight each other for a higher spiritual ranking. Instead, he encourages all of us to contend together for "the faith."

Be careful not to overlook how Jude wrote his appeal using *a plural "you"* and not singular. In an age when personal faith is considered so important, this points to an often disregarded reality. We need each other.

Only within a community of believers can God accomplish His work to help us grow in our faith and become the person He always intended for us to be. Paul assured us "that God, who began the good work within you, will continue His work until it is finally finished on the day when Christ Jesus returns" (Phil. 1:6, NLT). Paul did not write to an individual in the Philippian church—he also used a plural "you" to address all of us and not just one of us.

Paul's words encouraged my faith when I was discouraged. Philippians 1:6 helped me not give up because I knew God was still working to fulfill His plan in my life. For years I thought, *"God is not finished with me yet."* But then, the Holy Spirit taught me how my thinking was self-centered and little more than an excuse. My faith was dead, and I remained the same because I failed to let God accomplish His work in me through accountability with other believers.

God perfects us through relationships with each other within a community of faith. You and I cannot "contend for the faith" in a vacuum separated from other believers. Loving, trusting friendships provide us with the opportunity to both give and receive the help we all so desperately need for our faith to come alive.

Resurrected faith recognizes our need for each other. Only together can we come to know the first faith and live with loving obedience to Jesus.

The Identity of a Contender

Before encouraging us to "contend for the faith," Jude first reminded us of our shared identity *in Christ*. We contend together based upon what Jesus accomplished for us and not what we try to do for ourselves. We are contenders based upon who God declared us to be in His Word. You and I cannot make ourselves a contender through human effort—it's not about what we say or think about ourselves. We contend for the faith because of who we are in Christ.

Jude wants us to be confident of our identity as contenders. Notice how he addressed those he wrote to, and in turn, each of us at the beginning of his short epistle. He writes, "To all who have been called by God the Father, who loves you and keeps you safe in the care of Jesus Christ. May God give you more and more mercy, peace, and love" (Jude 1:1-2, NLT).

First century believers did not have a printed copy of Jude's letter to read, like we do today, but listened as it was read or recited. The oral tradition at that time impacted how Jude wrote his letter. Because his audience did not have a personal copy of his letter, Jude used two triplets to state the identity of believers in a way they could remember it. He built the second triplet upon the first for emphasis, like underlining or highlighting what he wrote in the oral tradition.

111

We are blessed to have Jude's letter printed and available to read anytime. However, English translators often change Jude's original word order in Greek and lose the emphasis and connection within his triplets. A rough word-for-word translation of Jude's salutation would be something like this: *To those in God the Father the BELOVED, and for Christ Jesus KEPT, the CALLED. To you, MERCY, PEACE, and LOVE be multiplied.*

To help people remember what he wrote, Jude began and ended the identity of a contender with two forms of love, first as a verb and then a noun. The activity of God's love establishes and completes who we are in Christ—the love of God is everything. Your identity begins and ends with God's absolute and unconditional love for you.

You and I will grasp how the LORD sees us as we consider the six parts of Jude's unbroken circle of love. We begin here with the first triplet that describes the contender's identity as the adored, protected, and chosen of God. Then in the next chapter, "Unfailing Confidence," we will examine the second triplet to see how our identity is unshakable and secure.

The Adored of God

Jude identifies us as those who are the "beloved in God the Father" (Jude 1:2). "Beloved" is not a word we often use today. It sounds old-fashioned, but we might benefit from its meaning. One's wholehearted expression of love makes the recipient your beloved— even if they do nothing to deserve it. Such is the case for you and me.

The verb translated "beloved," written in the Greek perfect passive tense, tells us three important things.[3] First, the perfect tense describes a single act of love with no need for repetition. Second, the expression of love continues with full effect into the present—it does not diminish or fail. Third, the passive voice shows the lover's activity, who initiates and completes the loving action without any contribution from the beloved.[4]

As the Father's beloved, God powerfully demonstrated His love when Jesus died in our place, a single loving initiative with unfailing force and effectiveness today. Furthermore, we are God's beloved by the wholehearted pursuit of God and not as the result of anything we said or did.

My wife, Susie, and I love each other with all our hearts. Our love is far from perfect, but, in a small way, it illustrates the magnitude of God's love for us. The foundation of our love grows from the commitment we made to each other and is not based upon anything we did to earn each other's love. We chose each other and sealed our choice with a single expression of love spoken through vows of commitment before family and friends on our wedding day.

Like other married couples, we have experienced our share of difficulties. Still, I treasure Susie as *"My Bride,"* and she looks at me as her *"Honey."* Our love grows in response to the many ways we show love to each other. Sometimes our loving feelings were momentarily diminished by things we said or did, but our choice remained, and forgiveness followed. Today, nearly forty years later, our single act of love remains in effect, and with God's help, our commitment will continue "until death we do part."

Now consider the greatness of Jesus' love for us. No one can do anything to earn the right to be God's beloved. God loves everyone in the world equally. The LORD'S love for humanity does not change—His love never fails because "God is love" (1 John 4:8, 16).

As the Father's beloved, God's love for us does not grow greater nor diminish in response to anything we say or do—good or bad. Before we even thought of loving Him back, God took the initiative to express His constant abiding love. With a single act of love, God did what we were powerless to do for ourselves. God demonstrated His love once and for all because "while we were still sinners, Christ died for us" (Rom. 5:8).

We need to be careful not to forget we were Jesus' enemies and rebels against God. Long before we had any idea to believe or respond to the kindness of Jesus, the Father proved how much he loved us by sending His Son to rescue us. God took action to make us His beloved. "This is how God loved the world: He gave His one and only Son" (John 3:16, NLT).

Resurrected faith understands the LORD loved us anyway even though we didn't deserve it.

God's immeasurable act of love does something more. Christ's love declares our immense value because the greater price love pays, the greater the value of the one loved.

The price of engagement rings varies greatly, but some suggest a guideline to spend two months' salary on the symbol of your enduring love. Jesus gave us more than two months of His life—He paid the ultimate price by laying down His life. Jesus' death makes us God's most treasured possession. You see, it is not a question of what we think we are worth. God determined our value by the price He paid for us.

The LORD paid such a great price for us as His beloved because He adores us—God sees in us what all too often we don't. We were created "in the image of God" (Gen. 1:27). Sin distorted God's likeness within us and makes it hard for us to see, but the Father still sees Himself in us. We are incredibly valuable to God—more than anything else in creation—because we bear His image.

Resurrected faith is stronger than feelings of worthlessness comprehending our great value as the "beloved in God the Father."

Consider our worth from Jesus' familiar story of a man with two sons—we know the younger as the prodigal son.[5] We are accustomed to viewing this story from the standpoint of the younger son leaving home with money in his pocket because we identify with him the most. We know what it's like to chase our dreams. Rather than be confined by our father's wishes, we take our inheritance to do our own thing. When everything is lost, we identify with the son's feeling of total worthlessness in his father's eyes. On the long journey home, we, too, rehearse the line over and over, "Father...I am no longer worthy to be called your son..." (Luke 15:18-19).

But think about this parable from the perspective of the father. When the son leaves home with his share of the inheritance, the father is right to be brokenhearted—his son treated him as if he were already dead. But the prodigal's rejection does not lessen the love of the father. With compassion, he begins a daily search of the horizon to see if his son is on the road coming home. Months pass, or perhaps years, but the father never loses hope. Each day he continues looking for his son. The day the father longs for finally comes. When he sees the boy in the distance, the father does not wait but runs down the road to welcome his son home with kisses and an embrace.

The son is taken back—this is not the sort of greeting the young man expected. The prodigal does his best to communicate his planned speech, but the father turns a deaf ear to the pitiful cry, "I'm unworthy." The father does not see the filth of a pig pen or a lowly servant. Instead, the father sees himself again in the face of his son.

Our heavenly Father is the father in Jesus' story. When we turn our heart's in repentance toward home, our Father sees. God runs to meet us on the road showering us with hugs and kisses. The LORD does not see us as unworthy sinners. The Father sees His image in us and welcomes us home as His child.

John was right—the Father showered His love upon us to call us His sons and daughters.[6] God made an extravagant expression of love to restore in us what He saw all along. In Christ, we can again reflect God's glory in and through our lives.

Jude identified us first as the "beloved in God the Father." Jesus' unfailing love continues to work in us to reveal His image and make God known to the world. Even when we stumble and fall, His love does not waver because "the LORD is merciful and gracious, slow to anger and abounding in steadfast love" (Ps. 103:8).

God's love for us "keeps no record of wrongs," and it "never fails" (1 Cor. 13:5, 8, NIV). More than likely, we all need this reminder—God's love does not change based upon what you or I might do or not do.

Resurrected faith is stronger than feelings of worthlessness comprehending our great value as the "beloved in God the Father."

The Protected of God

God protects and keeps us safe because we are the Father's "beloved" uniquely identified as the LORD'S treasured possession. Each of us has things important to us. Whether these items only have sentimental value or possess inherent worth, we safeguard them.

Jude continues with a logical progression to identify contenders as those "kept for Christ Jesus" (Jude 1:2). The verb "kept" was also written as a perfect passive like "beloved" and would be better translated as "continually kept." The LORD acted once to provide unfailing protection for us—the fortification and welfare He gave remains always in full effect.[7]

Jesus worked to keep us constantly safe and secure. He called Himself our Good Shepherd who willingly "lays down His life for the sheep," holding nothing back to protect His sheep (John 10:11). In this way, Jesus gives His sheep eternal life, so they will never be harmed because no one can take them out of His hand.

Sheltered within the hands of Jesus, nothing can hurt us—not even death.

We must learn to appreciate our identity as the adored and protected of God, so we can stand together and "contend for the faith." In his fight for faith, the Apostle Paul experienced incredible difficulty, being imprisoned, beaten, pelted with rocks, shipwrecked multiple times, left for dead, and more.[8] Yet through it all, he never wavered, knowing he was secure in Christ.

Mindful of his security, Paul asked Christians in Rome questions we should ponder today. Aware of how easily fear paralyzes believers, he asked, "if God is on our side, then tell me: whom should we fear?" (Rom. 8:31, VOICE). The obvious answer is no one, but we often give in to anxiety and terror of all kinds. Paul continued, "What can come between us and the love of God's Anointed? Can troubles, hardships, persecution, hunger, poverty, danger, or even death?" He answered immediately, "absolutely nothing" (verse 35). By the great love of Jesus, we are without a doubt absolutely and altogether protected by God.

Paul encouraged believers to move beyond acknowledging truth with their heads by an intellectual agreement to abiding in peaceful rest through the God-given assurance within their hearts. Unexpected trials may flood our minds with doubts and questions about God's care, but our hearts stand firm in Christ. Like Paul, we remain confident lifting a crescendo of praise that absolutely nothing in all creation "can come between us and the love of God revealed in the Anointed, Jesus our LORD" (Rom. 8:39, VOICE).

Resurrected faith does not ignore one's circumstances or trials but is grounded in the unshakeable reality of God's keeping power. Living faith walks confidently with Jesus through difficulty and with an eternal perspective lifts your gaze to see Jesus' protective, unfailing love.

In his first epistle, the Apostle John shows us how the protective power of Christ Jesus our LORD completely transforms how we live. John says God's children will no longer continue to "make a practice of sinning, for God's Son holds them securely, and the evil one cannot touch them" (1 John 5:18, NLT). We have no more excuses for sin or thinking, *"The devil made me do it"* because we are untouchable in Jesus' hands.

We might be inclined to disagree with John because we know all too well how we continue to struggle with sin. However, an awareness of our security in Christ sets us free from habitual sin because "anyone who belongs to God's family will be unable to maintain a continual practice of sin."[9] You and I can overcome every temptation because the enemy can't touch us—we're safe in Jesus' hands.

We all need this reminder because we're quick to forget who we are, but living faith enables us to rest securely through our identity as God's protected.

Satan wants to lead you into sin by convincing you Jesus won't give you the best life can offer. Don't yield to temptation like Adam and Eve, believing the lie God is holding out on you. The LORD will provide everything you need. You are free from the cares and worries of life because Jesus holds you safely in His hands.

In the real world, sin makes life messy. You and I know believers who struggle with sin—sometimes it's the person staring back at us in the mirror. Our place is not to judge Christians who sin as not being a child of God. Instead, Jesus wants to use us to help restore each other with gentleness, cautious not to be similarly taken captive.[10] The Father knows His children, and Jesus stands ready to protect and support everyone who looks to Him for help to overcome every temptation.

Encourage other Christians not to lose sight of who they are as believers. In the hands of Jesus, we are completely safe, and the enemy won't be able to lead us astray. Protection is ours because it is our sure identity as those "kept [by] Christ Jesus."[11]

We all need this reminder because we're quick to forget who we are, but living faith enables us to rest securely through our identity as God's protected.

The Chosen of God

Beloved by the Father and kept by Christ Jesus, Jude completes his triplet, reminding us we are "the called" (Jude 1:1).[12] God's love and protection forever impact our identity as the chosen, not because of anything we did or can do, but because of what the LORD did on our behalf. Our identification as those "who are the called" means we are called, invited, divinely selected, and appointed by God.[13]

We understand what it means to receive a call. When we were children, our mothers shouted our names to come in for dinner, or today, someone might call or text us on the phone. The voice, chime, ringtone, or another summons for our attention demands a reaction— we stopped playing and came into the house or answered the phone. You and I are accustomed to responding when someone calls us, even if we ignore their call.

Being those "who are the called" of God is not like that at all.

The way Jude wrote this points to something more profound. He began with two perfect verbs showing the activity of God to make us His beloved and kept ones. Used as an adjective, "called" described the believers Jude wrote to and, in turn, all of us today. In this way, we are "divinely summoned" based solely upon the LORD'S initiative and not our answer.[14] By divine invitation, we are called to God, Himself in the person of Jesus.[15]

God does not call us because of our ability or position. Instead, in His love, we are called in spite of ourselves.

By the Spirit's power, the work of "*faithing*" begins its work in us through the hearing of God's word—the divine invitation. "*Faithing*" completes its work to quicken our hearts with believing faith to respond and answer God's call to be saved.

Paul used a similar greeting when writing to the church in Rome. He identified believers as those "who are loved by God and called to be saints" (Rom. 1:7). Like Jude, Paul described followers of Jesus in three ways—they are beloved, called, and saints. Our identity as saints does not mean we have glowing halos around our heads, or the church promoted us to sainthood. Being recognized as saints means we are holy ones, set apart to God.[16]

Deep within our hearts, all of us have a desire to be accepted. We want to know we belong and are not an outsider. I remember being picked for a neighborhood baseball, basketball, or football game. While seldom first, I was glad not to be the last one chosen. No one envied those at the end of the line. Unwanted by either team, captains often argued back and forth, "You take him…No, I don't want him. You take him."

Both Jude and Paul declared good news! You are not *"the unwanted."* The LORD does not overlook or turn you away. You are valuable. God's desire is for you to be His very own. The Father in heaven looked upon you with favor, speaks your name, and calls you His very own.

Jesus told His disciples, "You did not choose me, but *I chose you*" (John 15:16, emphasis mine). Like the disciples, you are not overlooked or unwanted because you don't measure up to your self-imposed standard. God does not call us because of our ability or position. Instead, in His love, we are called in spite of ourselves.[17]

The LORD sets us apart as the chosen of God and identifies us for all eternity as the "called."

Jesus took the initiative to make us "those who are called, beloved in God the Father and kept" by Him (Jude 1:1). The love, protection, and calling of Jesus bring us from death to life. When we understand who we are in Christ, we are transformed from the inside out. The next chapter will reveal how we can live what we believe with multiplied certainty.

Resurrected faith animates the unchanging reality of our God-given identity.

Contending for Resurrected Faith

✝ Resurrected faith does not strive to be somebody but recognizes Jesus accepts us like little children.

- o Therefore, we refuse to believe the lie we are not good enough for God, and
- o We do not give in to thinking too highly of ourselves or the self-centered belief we are better than other people.

✝ The heart of a contender recognizes we come to God just as we are, but we do not come alone.

- o Superficial connections with other believers give way to loving and trusting friendships.
- o God wants us to contend within a community of believers built upon authentic and accountable relationships.

✝ We contend together for "the faith" based upon our shared identity in Christ.

✝ We contend as the beloved of God who took the initiative to prove His love even when we were still His enemies.

✝ We struggle together as the protected of God with full knowledge Christ acted on our behalf to keep us safe and secure.

✝ We take our stand for the faith not because of anything we did, but because the LORD called us as His own—we are the chosen and appointed by God.

Notes Chapter 6 "The Contender's Identity"

[1] Westfall, Carter. "What does it mean when Ophelia says…" Enotes.com. (June 23, 2015), Accessed April 11, 2020. https://www.enotes.com/homework-help/ophelia-says-lord-we-know-what-we-are-hamlet-125045

[2] Seuss, Dr. Happy Birthday to You. New York, NY: Random House Children's Books, 1987.

[3] Jude used *ēgapēmenois* the perfect, passive, plural from of the Greek verb *agapaō* or love. Again, the plural points to our being in a community of believers and not merely loved individually by God. I love each of my five children, but they are together loved with the same unconditional love—my beloved. Jude 1:1 :: English Standard Version (ESV) Interlinear. BlueLetterBible.org. Accessed June 18, 2018. https://www.blueletterbible.org/esv/jde/1/1/p0/t_concf_1167001

[4] Keating, Corey. Greek Verbs (Shorter Definitions). NTGreek.org. Accessed November 19, 2019. https://www.ntgreek.org/learn_nt_greek/verbs1.htm

[5] See Luke 15:11-24.

[6] See 1 John 3:1.

[7] The Greek verb *tetērēmenois* translated "kept" was written as a perfect, passive, plural. Jude 1:1 :: English Standard Version (ESV) Interlinear., and Keating.

[8] See 2 Corinthians 11:23-27.

[9] 1 John 5:18 restates what was stated in 1 John 3:9,"No one born of God makes a practice of sinning." Harris, Ralph W. (General Editor). *The New Testament Study Bible: Hebrews - Jude.* Springfield, MO: The Complete Biblical Library. 1989. pp. 393, 429.

[10] See Galatians 6:1-2; 1 John 5:16-18.

[11] Translation from one language to another is never word for word. In the Greek neither the conjunction *gar* often translated "for" nor the preposition *en* translated "in" or "by" appear in Jude's original text. Instead "Jesus Christ" was written in the dative case, which is translated differently based upon the context. Among the several possibilities "for," "by," or "in" are among the most frequent words used to translate the dative. Many English translations like the ESV and NIV choose "kept for Jesus Christ" but indicate the other possible translations by way of a footnote. Greek Case. BCBSR.com. Accessed June 15, 2018. http://www.bcbsr.com/greek/gcase.html

[12] Jude 1:1 :: English Standard Version (ESV) Interlinear.

[13] Lexicon :: Strong's G2822 – Kletos. BlueLetterBible.org. Accessed December 18, 2018. https://www.blueletterbible.org/lang/lexicon/lexicon.cfm?Strongs=G2822&t=ESV

[14] Harris. p. 457.

[15] "Called," from the Greek word *klētos*, was written in the dative case. In general, the dative case answers one of three questions: To/For whom? How? or Where? The perfect passive verbs "beloved" and "kept" answer the how question clearly pointing to the activity of God that endures with full effect to the present. Thus, the dative case of

124

"called" answers the to/for whom question, which is God's calling to Himself in Christ. (Greek Case n.d.)

[16] Lexicon :: Strong's G40 - Hagios. BlueLetterBible.org. Accessed December 18, 2018. https://www.blueletterbible.org/lang/lexicon/lexicon.cfm?Strongs=G40&t=ESV

[17] See 1 Corinthians 1:26-31.

Chapter 7

Unfailing Confidence

*In the fear of the LORD one has strong
confidence, and his children will have a refuge.*

Proverbs 14:26 (ESV)

In the last inning of the season's final game, I walked to home plate with dad's words echoing in my mind, "Swing the bat and see what happens." This at-bat was my final chance as a seven-year-old "rookie" to get a hit.

During my inaugural season playing baseball, I got on first base lots of times. Either the umpire said, "Ball four, take your base," or I

Being told who we are is not enough—we need the unfailing seven-year-old confidence to live the identity Jesus gave us.

got hit by an eight-year-old's wild pitch. However, I also struck out a lot. Going down swinging was not my style. No, I held my bat firmly over my shoulder, watching strike three fly into the catcher's mitt.

At practice, I got more than my share of hits when the coach pitched—I even got on base when he said, "Okay, run this one out." But, alas, on game day, I froze when the opposing pitcher stared me down.

This time would be different. I took my practice swings and faced the pitcher. Unfortunately, I needed a longer bat for my attempt to hit the first pitch because the ball sailed far outside, and the catcher had to retrieve it from the backstop. Strike one. Standing in the batter's box, I saw my mom cheering me on from the bleachers. Swing and a miss, strike two.

If the pitcher knew I was determined to swing at every pitch, he would have thrown that last ball far outside again. He didn't. I swung as hard as I could, and the ball hit the bat. I ran to first base, and the coach pointed for me to keep going to second as the ball sailed over the centerfielder's head. I saw the third base coach signal me to keep running. My coach stopped me at third, but I was sure I could have beaten the relay throw to home and made it a home run.

I got lots more hits in the following seasons—home runs too. Moving out of rightfield, where I chased more butterflies than fly balls, I took my position at first and second base in the infield. But, I'll never forget my first real hit because something changed in me that day.

Win or lose, our coach told us after every game, "You guys are great ballplayers." So, with my first hit, I believed him. Deep down, I had confidence empowering me to be a ballplayer.

As believers, we are more than ballplayers. Jude told us we are the adored, chosen, and protected of God. However, being told who we are is not enough—we need the unfailing seven-year-old confidence to live out the identity Jesus gave us.

An Unshakable Identity

Our identity in Christ is established once and for all, but Jude did not want us to think, *"This sounds too good to be true! How can we be the beloved, kept, and called of God?"* And so, Jude continued with a second triplet, a prayer for believers to have a multiplied certainty of who we are in Christ Jesus. He did not want anyone to forget their God-given identity, praying, "May mercy, peace, and love be multiplied to you" (Jude 1:2).

Remember, in the oral tradition, Jude's repetition of triplets beginning and ending with love acted to highlight his words and underscore their God-given identity. In this way, Jude helped his listeners not forget who they are in Christ. Thus, Jude prays for the beloved to receive ever-increasing mercy, the kept to inherit abundant overflowing peace, and the called to have love lavished upon them without measure.

The LORD continues to answer Jude's ancient prayer today, placing unfailing confidence within the hearts of contenders, like you and me.

Limitless Mercy

Jude asked for the multiplication of mercy upon those who are the beloved of God. The LORD'S nature and very essence is love.[1] Little wonder the Psalmist tells us how the God of love does not respond in anger to our sin or punish us for our willful disobedience because "as high as the heavens are above the earth, so great is His mercy for those who fear Him" (Ps. 103:11, TLV).

The love of God extends His limitless mercy to us. In scripture, the Hebrew word for "mercy" is also translated as "love," "steadfast love," "unfailing love," "lovingkindness," and "kindness." Based upon concrete actions, mercy can be pictured as "bowing the neck to another as a sign of kindness."[2] Therefore, the LORD'S lovingkindness is not an act of weakness. On the contrary, God displays omnipotent strength through mercy to provide favor and protection to all who believe.

Our sin warrants punishment with the full vengeance of God's wrath, but from the cross, Jesus bowed His head, looking at us with kindness we did not deserve. The LORD extends His infinite mercy to us rather than the just penalty of death for our sins.

The first use of "mercy" in scripture provides a clear picture of how God extends His kindness to those unworthy of it. In Genesis 19, the LORD'S angels came to Sodom and Gomorrah. According to the custom at that time, Abraham's nephew, Lot, welcomed them into the safety of his home. The men of the city were not as hospitable. Instead, they revealed their wickedness that night. With uncontrolled sexual lust, they surrounded Lot's home demanding his guests be given to them to satisfy their evil desires.

Resurrected faith rests in the work Jesus did for us, confident we are the beloved of God with mercy multiplied over and over to us.

What Lot did next exposed the sinful condition of his heart— he offered his virgin daughters to them for their pleasure. Lot was quick to protect the strangers he just welcomed into his home. But to maintain his standing in the community, Lot was willing to hand over the daughters he loved and raised to be defiled and raped.

The men of the city were not so easily appeased. They despised Lot for making himself their judge. They would have attacked and possibly killed Lot if the angels had not blinded them and pulled him back into his house.

The LORD showed mercy to Lot because of Abraham's intercession on behalf of the righteous. The angels told Lot to flee with his family to the mountains to escape the destruction of the unrighteous who lived in the city. Lot responded to the angels, "Your servant has found favor in your eyes, and you have shown great kindness [or mercy] to me in sparing my life" (Gen. 19:19).

At that moment, Lot recognized his sin. Years earlier, his uncle suggested their camps move in different directions because their servants were quarreling. Lot looked with longing toward the fertile Jordan Valley. He chose to pitch his tent with the men of Sodom even though they were "extremely wicked and constantly sinned against the LORD" (Gen. 13:13, NLT). Lot realized he deserved to die with the rest of the inhabitants of Sodom and Gomorrah. But he was overcome by God's limitless mercy toward him and his family when the angels told him to flee the city.

God looked upon Lot with favor to spare his life and bring him under the LORD'S protection even though he did not deserve it.

The LORD'S rescue of Lot went far beyond Abraham's request for mercy.[3] Abraham did not simply ask the LORD to refrain from destroying his nephew. He negotiated with God. First, he asked to relent for the sake of fifty righteous people. Gradually, Abraham reduced the number until God agreed to his request to spare the city for the sake of only ten righteous. In the end, only four so-called righteous were found—Lot, his wife, and two daughters. The LORD exceeded Abraham's request because His mercy is greater than His wrath.

The limitless mercy of Jesus is likewise abundantly given to us as well. In love, He bore our sin upon the cross, freely giving forgiveness and grace we don't deserve. But God's love did not stop there. With multiplied mercy, Jesus rescued us from the death penalty, rightfully ours, and provided the gift of eternal life in its place.

Dead faith acknowledges God's love but fails to comprehend how Jesus multiplies His love in mercy. Lifeless belief is empty but continues to try to balance the scale. Without the confidence of their God-given identity, those with dead faith try to do enough good works to earn God's love.

Resurrected faith rests in the work Jesus did for us, confident we are the beloved of God with mercy multiplied to us over and over.

Steadfast Peace

Followers of Jesus are the kept, secure within the LORD'S hands, so Jude prayed they might also be the beneficiaries of God's abiding peace. The absence of conflict was not Jude's request. Instead, he prayed for contenders to experience the unshakeable peace of God even through life's most difficult trials and turmoil.

On the night of Jesus' betrayal, He was with His disciples and prepared them for what was about to happen. Jesus gave them the promise of God's unfailing peace, saying, *"Peace I leave with you; my peace I give you...*Do not let your hearts be troubled and do not be afraid"* (John 14:27, emphasis mine).

Jesus knew fear would soon overwhelm His disciples. Their world would be turned upside down—scattered, like sheep without a shepherd. So, the LORD tried to prepare them for what was about to happen, telling His disciples how much the world hated Him and would likewise hate them. But, unfortunately, they failed to grasp all Jesus said to them.

Before going to Gethsemane, where the God-ordained events would begin to unfold, Jesus again reassured His disciples. He said, "I have told you these things, so that in me *you may have peace.* In this world you will have trouble. But take heart! I have overcome the world" (John 16:33, emphasis mine).

Today, we need to hear and understand the rich promise for us in Jesus' words.

Not once, but twice Jesus promised the disciples His unfailing peace to keep them through the most challenging and unimaginable trials. However, the LORD's peace was not for them alone. And, so, with unwavering confidence, Jude prayed for everyone kept secure in the hands of Christ Jesus to rest in His multiplied peace.

Our perception of peace needs to expand. Peace means more than the absence of conflict or turmoil, and contrary to our western way of thinking, peace is not an abstract idea. Peace is much more than a feeling of inner calm or state of mind we try to obtain through meditation. Peace means more than the end of fighting and strife.

We need our thinking about peace to align with a biblical worldview. The Jewish understanding of peace comes from the Hebrew word *shalom*. While typically translated as peace, *shalom* "literally means 'to make whole,'" and is a concrete reality and completeness that can be given and received.[4]

In the first century, Jews understood peace as the substance of who we are—it's a reality of our personhood. So, when Jesus said, *"my peace I give you"* and *"in me you may have peace,"* He gives the fullness of Himself—Jesus promises wholeness, lacking nothing to all who follow Him.

In answer to Jude's prayer for multiplied peace in the lives of believers, Jesus gives of Himself to us in the same way. Thus, the LORD imparts His peace and wholeness abundantly to us as those securely kept in Christ.

Living faith makes us whole in the LORD. As a result, we receive God's perfect peace. A peace that makes us complete and overflows with well-being into every area of our lives. This *shalom* peace brings spiritual, emotional, mental, and physical health. However, God's peace does not stop with just personal inner peace.

The peace of Christ is alive within us to make us a peacemaker. With resurrected faith, the peace we receive from God is active and multiplied in all our relationships. Family, friends, and even acquaintances can be the recipient of peace, so they, too, might be made whole.

We have all been there. The victim and the culprit of stolen peace. God never intended for it to be that way.

The LORD'S peace holds us securely in the hands of Jesus, so we lack nothing. Christ alone gives His complete wholeness to us, and then with multiplied certainty, empowers us to bring His peace into the lives of others. With resurrected faith, we realize we should not just selfishly long for peace in our lives. Instead, abundant, unending peace is received and shared freely to transform our world.

An awakening to how sharing the peace of Christ we receive with others should also cause us to realize how the enemy seeks to use people and circumstances to rob us and others of the LORD'S peace.[5] How sobering for us to grasp, we can either be an individual who shares or steals peace from others.

Often insignificant things rob us of the peace Jesus gives. For example, we feel pressure at work to meet a deadline. Our lunch was not prepared right. We can't connect to the internet, so we use the hotspot on our phone, but then the battery dies. Traffic is stop-and-go on the highway. Any one of these or countless others can cause us to get upset. Yet, these are just possible mishaps of today. Our anxiety and fear about tomorrow make us our own worst enemy, losing sleep and stealing away the peace we need.

Unfortunately, the enemy works overtime to continue stealing away peace. Not only do we let little things rob us of our peace, but growing frustration and a bad attitude often cause us to take peace from others. We make sarcastic jokes tearing people down, or a stranger becomes the target of an unkind rebuke. Pent-up frustration boils over on undeserving family and friends.

We have all been there. The victim and the culprit of stolen peace. God never intended for it to be that way.

Jude identified us as those who are "kept for Jesus Christ," so he prayed that we would be the recipients of multiplied peace. We are the protected of God with the LORD'S peace—an overflowing abundance of unbroken wholeness.

With resurrected faith and overflowing peace, we can obey Jesus' command to "not worry about tomorrow...[because] living faithfully is a large enough task for today" (Matt. 6:34, VOICE).

Unending Love

The "beloved" receive God's mercy. The "kept" have the LORD'S peace, and the "called" are the chosen beneficiaries of the Father's unending love. Jude wants us to see how our identity begins and ends with love. We are loved and known by God because "God is love" (1 John 4:8).

The apostle Paul described love in 1 Corinthians 13. These words are often read at weddings or included on greeting cards for family and friends. Yet, we sometimes miss or forget that Paul's description of love is also an excellent portrayal of God. Consider how our heavenly Father's love is multiplied to us as the "called."

The indescribable love of God toward us is beyond measure.

Paul began saying, "Love is patient, love is kind." God does not look at his watch and get grumpy because we keep Him waiting, nor does God lash out because we disappointed Him. Paul continued saying love "does not envy, it does not boast, it is not proud. It does not dishonor others, it is not self-seeking, it is not easily angered, it keeps no record of wrongs." God is not selfish, demanding His way or the highway. God doesn't lose His cool and lash out in anger when we disappoint Him, nor does the LORD keep score but is ready to forgive. Paul concluded by saying, "Love does not delight in evil but rejoices with the truth. It always protects, always trusts, always hopes, always perseveres. Love never fails" (1 Cor. 13:4-8, NIV). God sees the best in us with unwavering confidence and won't give up just because we stumble and fall. God will never abandon us but watches over us and keeps us from harm. God has big dreams for all of His children and encourages us not to give up. God's love is never distant—it will never grow cold. No matter what happens, God's love endures through thick or thin.

In this way, we see how genuine love becomes a portrait of God's very essence and nature. Therefore, to know God is to know true love. And so, because love never fails, God never fails.[6]

Unfortunately, some people don't know God this way. Rather than see God as loving, they believe the lie God is always angry with them. Some believe God rejects them because they are not good enough. Life's disappointments and hardships affirm their misguided thinking that God didn't come through or failed them somehow. If only they would for a moment grasp how much God loves them.

The indescribable love of God toward us is beyond measure. Yet, if we were somehow able to gauge the Father's love, we would discover God cannot love us more nor love us less.

God is not distant but welcomes us to embrace Him as our Father with outrageous love. To approach God like this should blow our minds! Stop for a moment to "consider the kind of extravagant love the Father has lavished on us—He calls us children of God! It's true; we are His beloved children" (1 John 3:1, VOICE). God made us His children giving us an unshakable identity as His beloved. Despite anything we may have said or done, God took the initiative to work on our behalf and make us His children.

Susie and I are blessed with five children and six grandchildren. Each time a baby was expected, that little one was loved long before being born. With our hearts overflowing with anticipation, hopes, and dreams, we loved each child simply for who they were. None needed to do anything to earn our love. Each child and grandchild is the recipient of our unconditional love.

If you ever expected a baby, whether by pregnancy or adoption, then you understand this unconditional love for a child. And, even if you only celebrate with family and friends expecting a baby, you probably recognize this kind of love.

The love and acceptance of a newborn is only a fraction of God's infinite love for us. Our heavenly Father does not love us because we have loved Him. God just loves us—period.

Many people have not acknowledged the LORD'S love, but God still loves them unconditionally. Regardless of how dirty sin makes them or the baggage they carry, God won't turn off His love. So, you and I need to stop keeping our distance, trying to clean ourselves up, and working to earn God's love. God proved His unfailing love for us even when we were still His enemies.[7]

The circle is complete—our identity begins and ends with God's love for us.

> *Resurrected faith does not contend for a creed or doctrine. Instead, we aim to know Jesus and grow to love Him more as we grasp, little by little, the unimaginable greatness of His love for us.*

Resurrected faith does not contend for a creed or doctrine. Instead, we aim to know Jesus and grow to love Him more as we grasp, little by little, the unimaginable greatness of His love for us.

Multiplied Certainty

Look again at how Jude identified those to whom he wrote and his prayer for them. "I am writing to all who have been called by God the Father, who loves you and keeps you safe in the care of Jesus Christ" (Jude 1:1-2, NLT). As followers of Jesus, this is our identity too. Jude's desire was for all believers to know their true selves. He prayed Jesus would give them a multiplied certainty of their identity with no room for doubt.

We limit God by thinking only in terms of addition. We might think God added three things to get three more things. Start with a bit of love, add some kept, plus a call equals a little more mercy, peace, and love.

God does not do addition—the LORD is the God of exponential multiplication.

Consider the "X factor" of multiplication in how Jesus took a little boy's lunch and fed over five thousand people with only five loaves and two fish. Then, Jesus USED the "X factor" again when He fed four thousand with only seven loaves and a few fish. Jesus' "X factor" is far more than our addition minds comprehend.

Miracles of addition might have taken these lunches intended for one and fed ten or twelve. If we were one of the disciples, we would be happy to send everyone home and have a quiet fish dinner. But Jesus was not interested in sharing a simple miracle of addition. Instead, Jesus did incredible works of multiplication. With only a little, Jesus fed the five thousand men, and a second time, four thousand men. These multitudes did not include the number of women or children who also enjoyed a great picnic with so little.

However, there is more to the story. Each time the disciples gathered many baskets filled with leftovers—far more than the small amount of fish and bread they found, Jesus provided a bonus meal for them.[8]

In much the same way, Jude prayed Jesus would do an even greater work of multiplication. Before urging believers to "contend for the faith," he asked the LORD to give them an ever-increasing conviction of their undeniable identity. Today, Jesus continues to answer Jude's prayer in our lives. We are the "beloved in God the

Father" who receive His multiplied mercy. The "X factor" of perfect peace is reproduced in our lives because we are "kept for Jesus Christ." And the unbroken circle is complete because as those "who are called," we abound in God's multiplied love.

Resurrected faith lifts us out of our feelings of inferiority and insecurity with a heart filled with unfailing confidence of who we are in Christ.

We must understand the importance of this timeless identity for us as followers of Jesus in the twenty-first century. Understanding who we are in Christ changes everything. We don't just need added certainty—we need multiplied certainty.

Too many believers today suffer from an identity crisis. American culture tells us we aren't good enough because we need better and more in many different ways. The food we eat, the clothes we wear, the phone we have in our pocket, the car we drive, the house we live in, and countless other things need to be new and improved. As a result, many people find themselves buried in debt, trying to create an appearance of success and happiness—while hoping no one notices the rest of their broken and outdated things. Little wonder so many people are uncertain of who they are and feel unworthy of God's love.

We will not have the confidence to boldly stand and fight for "the faith" if we are unsure of our identity. We must be on guard and give no place to fear and worry that cripples us. The devil will try to deafen our ears to God's Word and whispers of the Holy Spirit. The enemy loudly shouts his lies of inferiority and words of condemnation. Our adversary seeks to blind us to the truth with a weak caricature of our God-given identity.

We should not be surprised that Satan tries to make us something we are not because even he masquerades "as an angel of light" (2 Cor. 11:14). Ask the Holy Spirit to awaken you each day with a reminder of who God made you as His child.

But, be careful not selfishly stop there. Jesus' work of multiplication goes beyond meeting only your needs. Jesus said, "You received these gifts freely, so you should give them to others freely" (Matt. 10:8, VOICE). We should join Jude's prayer for other believers to comprehend who they are in Christ with multiplied certainty. The Holy Spirit will empower us to encourage those still unsure of their identity to grow in confidence of their God-given identity.

We are the body of Christ. If one part suffers an identity crisis, we all suffer.[9] Similarly, the assurance of our shared identity strengthens our unity as members together in the body of Christ—knowing who we are will help keep us from schisms, being quick to forgive one another "just as in Christ God forgave [us]" (Eph. 4:32, NIV).

In chapter two, "A Crisis of Faith," we discovered how dead faith gives the false impression of life because our hearts are deceitful and desperately sick. One way the LORD works to resurrect faith within our hearts is by helping us to know our true identity.

The Holy Spirit empowers us with the confidence of who we are in Christ to live righteous lives. With living faith, we live more and more like Jesus. Resurrected faith aligns our identity with what we do and say every day, silencing the enemy's condemnation.

A watching world is not blind to the hypocrisy within the church—non-believers see our charade trying so hard to be someone we are not. Our dead faith religion paralyzes the gospel because no one wants to feel like they are never good enough in God's eyes.

The Holy Spirit wants to give us a multiplied certainty of our identity, so our faith becomes authentic. When we are confident of who we are in Christ, our witness will be effective, and people in our lives will come to know Jesus as their Savior and LORD. And in knowing Jesus, they also come to grasp their new identity and will be forever changed.

When we contend together for "the faith," we know Jesus and ourselves as He made us. Living faith gives us multiplied certainty of our identity and empowers us to:

- Stand firm against our adversary, the devil.
- Build up other believers in their God-given identity.
- Maintain unity in the body with loving forgiveness.
- Walk according to the Spirit and not the flesh.
- Share an authentic faith reproduced in the lives of those who do not yet know Jesus as Savior and LORD.

Resurrected faith lifts us out of our feelings of inferiority and insecurity with a heart filled with unfailing confidence in who we are in Christ. We are loved without measure, secure, and chosen as recipients of God's multiplied mercy, peace, and love.

Stop striving to become somebody and grasp who God made you to be in Jesus.

Contending for Resurrected Faith

✟ Resurrected faith gives us unfailing confidence in our identity in Christ.

✟ God's mercy provides us with multiplied certainty we are the Father's beloved.

  o Jesus does not treat us as our sins deserve but offers His lovingkindness.

  o Dead faith continually tries to balance the scale, while resurrected faith rests confidently in the LORD'S mercy.

✟ The peace of our LORD Jesus Christ gives us multiplied certainty we are kept securely in His hands.

  o Jesus gives us the fullness of Himself to impart His peace and wholeness in our lives.

✟ Rather than the absence of trials or turmoil, *shalom* peace is a concrete reality and completeness that can be given and received.

  o Resurrected faith also empowers us to share the peace Jesus gives to us with other people.

✟ As recipients of Jesus' wholeness, we are careful not to let the devil's schemes rob us of peace.

  o Resurrected faith also remains vigilant against the enemy's tactics, not allowing him to use us to steal peace from others.

✟ Our heavenly Father's love proves we are those called by God with multiplied certainty.

- o Genuine love provides a portrait of God because "God is love."

- o Living faith grasps how the Father lavishes His love upon us as His children because God cannot love us more nor love us less.

- o The circle of our identity is complete, beginning and ending as an unbroken circle of God's love for us.

- o The "X factor" of Jesus' multiplication produces an unfailing confidence in our true identity and makes all the difference in how we live our lives every day.

Notes Chapter 7 "Unfailing Confidence"

[1] See 1 John 4:8, 16.

[2] In the Hebrew the word *checed* is often translated "mercy" or "lovingkindness." See Benner, Jeff A. *Ancient Hebrew Dictionary*. College Station, TX: Virtualbookworm.com Publishing Inc. 2009. p. 338

[3] See Genesis 18:23-32.

[4] Benner, Jeff A. *The Living Words, Volume One*. College Station, TX: Virtualbookworm.com Publishing Inc. 2007. pp. 97-99

[5] See John 10:10

[6] See Zephaniah 3:5; 1 John 4:16.

[7] See Romans 5:8.

[8] See Matthew 14:13-21; 15:32-38.

[9] See 1 Corinthians 12:12, 26-27.

Chapter 8

The Heart of a Contender

*So be strong and courageous, all you who put
your hope in the LORD!*

Psalm 31:24 (NLT)

Within the heart of a contender is a drive to persevere. Regardless of the cost they won't throw in the towel or take the easy way out. Like a combatant, we joined an ongoing struggle "contend for the faith."

Now our first journey together comes to its final chapter. We have learned what it means for us to fight for resurrected faith. Jude's ancient yet timely call now resonates within us. God put within us the heart of a contender.

We discovered what faith is along the way, so we contend for the right thing. Faith is not the secular idea of an unprovable belief or something accepted blindly. Nor is faith the religious concept of ideal principles or a deity to guide our lives.

For many Christians, their understanding of faith develops from either the secular, religious, or some combination of these patterns of thinking. Unfortunately, these views are impotent and incapable of producing the life Jesus died to provide for us. The pandemic of dead faith keeps us from living a fruitful, joyful, and obedient life

Resurrected faith is alive and active with confidence to trust God in every area of our lives. Through the power of the Holy Spirit, the activity of *"faithing"* produces surrendered obedience to live what we believe. To say, "I trust in God" is one thing, but putting our money where our mouth is, well, that's something entirely different.

A team-building game we played years ago illustrates the work of *"faithing"* to transform our behavior. First, one person stood on a chair with arms crossed over their chest and back to the group. Then, six to eight team members were randomly chosen to stand in pairs with arms interlinked behind them. Next, the individual on the chair said, "Ready to fall," and the team responded, "Ready to catch." Finally, on the count of three, the person fell backward from the chair into the team's waiting arms.

Doing this sounds simple enough—until you stand on the chair, unable to see those you must trust to catch you.

I remember one young girl eager to take her place on the chair, but her confidence evaporated, and she stood frozen, unable to let herself fall. She got down and watched several others taller and heavier than her get caught. Finally, returning to the chair, she overcame her fear and fell into her team's arms with a joyful scream. When she stood frozen on the chair, her confidence was dead, but in time, her faith came alive to change her behavior.

With complete surrender, "faithing" will set you free from the ice-cold chill of dead faith to fall into the arms of Jesus.

The Holy Spirit wants to do the same work in our lives today. So don't remain frozen, living your life out of alignment with your stated belief in Jesus. Instead, allow the activity of faith to transform you from the inside out. With complete surrender, *"faithing"* will set you free from the ice-cold chill of dead faith to fall into the arms of Jesus.

"Faithing," the intersection of faith as a noun and a verb, is the Spirit's activity to write the doctrine of belief upon our hearts and then empower us to live out what we believe without contradiction. This work is not a one-time event but an ongoing process of sanctification, making us more like Jesus.

Four final reminders will help us not give up but persevere with the heart of a contender in our fight for resurrected faith. The simple ABCs outline presented here does not mean our struggle "to contend for the faith" will be easy. Instead, an elementary ABCs forms the framework to help us remain in the fight and remember our focus. We can secure our footing when we find ourselves overcome with uncertainty, fearful of trusting God, and unwilling to take the next step of faithful obedience to Jesus.

151

A. – Abide in Christ

Americans love things of all shapes and sizes. People claim to love lots of stuff like bikes, cars, movies, TV shows, pizza, tacos, sports teams, and more. Intuitively, they know these things cannot love them back, but they go on loving them anyway.

Even Christians make the same mistake. To think we can love something makes loving Jesus difficult because unknowingly, we reduce Him to an idea and not a person. To fall in love with a creed or doctrine about Jesus leaves us empty and longing for something more—yearning for someone who will love us back.

God gave you the heart of a contender with a deep growing love for Jesus. This love is real because, unlike the many things we love, Jesus not only loves us back, He loves us first. Therefore, the more we come to know the God who loves us in spite of ourselves, the more our love for the LORD grows.

Loving Jesus more means you no longer want to settle for one of the many caricatures of church doctrines about Him. You want to know Jesus and comprehend "the faith" He reveals through knowing Him. You decided to let Jesus define your beliefs and not allow church doctrines to confine Him in a theological box or make Him something He is not.

You responded to Jude's ancient yet timely plea to "contend for the faith." The struggle for resurrected faith is not to know a creed or doctrine. Instead, your passion is to know Jesus through His self-revelation of God beginning at creation and perfectly fulfilled when He put on human flesh. Jesus "is the radiance of the glory of God and [is] the exact imprint of His nature" (Heb. 1:3). With resurrected faith, Jesus opens our hearts to know and love God like never before.

How can our love for Jesus continue to grow, so we don't fall back into the religious routine of just knowing about God rather than truly knowing Him?

Those with dead faith neglect their connection to Jesus and other believers.

Abide in Christ. Never separate yourself from Jesus or compartmentalize your faith as one of many parts of your life. Instead, ask the LORD to increase your God-awareness to recognize how Jesus is with you always.

Jesus' words ring true for us today when He told the disciples, "Abide in me, and I in you…for apart from me you can do nothing" (John 15:4-5). Like them, we are branches depending upon Jesus, the vine, to provide all we need. Branches do not strain to produce fruit but receive life-giving nourishment from the vine.

Christians sometimes struggle to dwell continually in Christ because they overlook a vital part of abiding in Him. The key is not to abide alone—branches are united to the vine collectively and not individually. The Greek verb translated "abide" is plural. Jesus tells us we are all to abide together in Him. When we isolate ourselves from other believers, we are also, sooner or later, disconnected from the vine, Jesus.

Those with dead faith neglect their connection to Jesus and other believers. They work hard trying to live up to the ideals their doctrines teach but cannot produce the fruit of love, joy, and obedience only made possible by abiding in the vine. Hear Jesus' warning! He said these lifeless branches are gathered together, "thrown into the fire, and burned" (John 15:6).

Resurrected faith reproduces the life of Jesus in contenders' hearts as together we continue to abide in Him and He in us.

B. – Be What You Believe

Our journey together began recalling how the LORD first invited Abram to set out on a pilgrimage of faith. He set out fatherless with God's promise to make his descendants into a great nation in a new homeland. Along the way, the LORD changed his name from Abram, meaning exalted father,[1] to Abraham, father of a multitude.[2]

Few of us today would have patient faith like Abraham. On the contrary, our culture pushes us to pursue instant gratification in all areas of our lives. As a result, we want microwavable beliefs to receive all God's promises now. Our expectation would be for God to give us our promised child in a year or less, but Abraham waited twenty-five years until Isaac was born. Abraham's pilgrimage was long, but with perseverance, he "believed God and trusted in His promises, so God counted it to his favor as righteousness" (Gen. 15:6, VOICE).

The LORD'S declaration of righteousness does not mean Abraham never made any mistakes. If Abraham's right standing before God was based upon his performance, then he earned his place of favor. However, the LORD affirmed Abraham's righteousness through faith and not works.[3]

God never gave up on Abraham when he took a misstep and strayed from the right path. Instead, like a tent peg driven deeper into solid ground, the LORD strengthened Abraham's faith to uphold God's word in the way he lived.

The ultimate test of Abraham's faith shows how he learned from his failures to walk the path the LORD directed him to take no matter what the cost. Years after Isaac was born, God asked Abraham to offer him as a sacrifice. So, father and son made the journey to Mount Moriah. Along the way, Isaac asked why they did not bring a lamb for the burnt offering. Knowing he was to

Trials might occasionally cause us to stumble, but the LORD strengthens us in our weakness to prove our faith is genuine.

offer his son as the sacrifice, Abraham answered, "God will provide for Himself the lamb" (Gen. 22:8). You most likely know the rest of the story—as Isaac lay bound upon the altar and Abraham raised the knife to kill his son, the LORD called out to stop him. Then, God showed him a ram caught in a thicket they could offer as a sacrifice in Isaac's place.

Abraham's faith was alive within him, enabling him to live what he believed. He lived in faithful obedience to God, willing to sacrifice his beloved son Isaac. Ultimately, Abraham had confidence "God was able even to raise [Isaac] from the dead, from which, figuratively speaking, he did receive him back." (Heb. 11:19).

While we won't face anything like Abraham did with Isaac, God will still direct us into times of testing. Jesus never said following Him on a journey of faith would be easy. Yes, the LORD sometimes leads us in ways that are difficult and don't make sense. We might even question whether or not we did the right thing to step out in faith and follow Jesus.

God never tests our faith so that it will falter and fail. Trials might occasionally cause us to stumble, but the LORD strengthens us in our weakness to prove our faith is genuine. Then, like Abraham, we can look back and see how God enabled us through the activity of *"faithing"* to align our faith and actions. In this way, we remain on a path to live with faithful obedience to our beliefs.

Resurrected faith enables contenders' hearts to persevere through any test through the power of the Holy Spirit. The LORD strengthens us to continue the journey and be what we believe by how we live our lives with living faith.

C. – Common Salvation

Jude was eager to write about "our common salvation," but Matthew, Mark, Luke, and John already told the good news story of Jesus. While one can only imagine the perspective the half-brother of Jesus might have included in his gospel narrative, first century Christians knew Jesus' biography of His life, death, and resurrection. So, the Holy Spirit compelled Jude to urge believers "to contend for the faith."

One cannot fight for the faith without first embracing the gospel message. If someone has not accepted Jesus as their Savior and LORD, they remain either indifferent, opposed, or unaware of God's gift of grace. Therefore, only the redeemed can struggle for the faith.

Unfortunately, not all believers will take a stand today "to contend for the faith." Instead, the dead faith pandemic infecting the church causes them to respond like the lost. They, too, are unknowingly apathetic, antagonistic, or ignorant of believers' ongoing struggle.

What causes such unexpected responses by some Christians to our fight for "the faith?" Of course, the Holy Spirit wants to awaken us from our dead faith sleepwalk, so we are alert and appreciate "our common salvation." But unfortunately, we sometimes neglect any of three parts of Jesus' rescue mission to seek and save the lost— two common and one uncommon.

Common Sickness

First, we disregard Jesus' rescue mission, curing us of our previous suffering caused by a common sickness. All of us were once "dead in [our] transgressions and sins" (Eph. 2:1). We tend to forget what it was like to be in bondage to a cruel master and slaves to sin.[4]

Growing up in the church, I sometimes looked down on people who gave themselves to so-called "big sins." I didn't realize how easily someone could stumble and fall into life-controlling addictions, immorality, and wickedness until I found myself yielding to various supersize temptations. That's when I came to understand a statement often taken for granted. We are not sinners because we sin—we sin because *we are sinners.*

People trapped by things we consider "big sins" are not worse sinners than we are. Regardless of how evil expresses itself, all sins are the same in the LORD'S eyes because sin separates people from God and one another. Everyone is born a sinner and shares a universal illness, which only Jesus can cure.

With gratitude, resurrected faith remembers how Jesus healed our common sickness to sin—an infection that leads to certain death.

Thankfully, "our common salvation" came to our rescue through Jesus' gift of eternal life.

Common Side Effects

We neglect Jesus' rescue mission a second way by ignoring the common side effects of living in a fallen world. Dead faith causes some believers to think they are done with temptation because they don't struggle with those "big sins." However, this line of thinking is faulty in three significant ways. First, no one is above temptation because the devil even tempted Jesus, but He was victorious and disarmed the enemy's traps.[5] Second, Jesus understands our weakness because He was tempted in every way like us and is ready to help us in our time of need.[6]

Some Christians may acknowledge these first two reasons and even use them to bolster the idea they are no longer tempted to sin. However, the third reason unravels their overconfident thinking. The enemy uses the desires of living in a flesh and blood body as the basis for all temptation—we get thirsty, hungry, tired, long for companionship, seek out pleasure, and so much more. Thus, while our spirits are alive in Christ, our inborn desires of the flesh or human longings become the bait to entice us to sin.[7]

Ultimately these cravings create the tug-of-war between our spirit and the flesh. Non-believers don't feel this tension because their spirits are still dead in sin. However, our spirits come to life by faith through the power of the Holy Spirit in us. Therefore, we feel the struggle and must choose how we live our lives. Through the activity of "faithing," the Spirit enables us to live what we believe, satisfying our appetites in ways that honor God. On the other hand, our flesh wants to give in to its various desires, sometimes with little or no thought, indulging carefree with unrestrained passions.

"Our common salvation" reminds us we must be careful not to forget the common side effects of living in a fallen world used by the enemy to lure us back into sin. Jesus rescued us, giving us victory over every temptation, so we can live our lives more and more like Him as we walk by the Spirit and not the flesh.

Uncommon Cure

The third way we neglect Jesus' rescue mission occurs through the misuse of the uncommon cure provided for the disease of sin. Jesus extends an extraordinary act of love to us, making "our common salvation" possible. So, to lose sight of the uncommon cure does not mean we necessarily forget the cross or the price Jesus paid for our forgiveness. Instead, we sometimes fail to appropriately apply God's grace to how we live our lives.

Of all the various world religions, only Christianity points to the finished work of Jesus as the means of salvation. Other belief systems require individuals to do something to earn salvation, enlightenment, peace in this life, or hope for a better afterlife. But as Christians, our hope comes from what Jesus accomplished on our behalf and not anything we can do to earn it.

Jesus provides an uncommon cure because God gives the gift of salvation by grace through faith—an undertaking no one else could ever accomplish.[8] Unfortunately, too many Christians squander God's amazing grace.

Christians claim to believe one receives salvation by grace through faith, but unfortunately, countless believers abandon God's grace once saved. Instead, they spend the rest of their lives trying to secure God's favor and stay saved through what they do. Far too many Christians keep score of the good and bad things they do, hoping to tip the scale in their favor—if not in God's eyes, then at least in the eyes of other churchgoers. In their eyes, achievements prove their faithfulness, so they never stop doing, earning, striving, and working. The forgot no one earns salvation by works, so all these do-gooders' deeds count for nothing.

Grace through faith alone provides and sustains our salvation—no one can begin to gain with accomplishments what God freely gives in Christ. Dead faith works harder, but resurrected faith exhales human effort, breathing in the breath of life.

Allow Jesus to resurrect your faith. Then you can respond to the present reality of His invitation to come and find real and lasting rest.[9] *"Faithing"* is not the redoubling of our efforts to do the right thing or create a checklist of dos and don'ts. Instead, *"faithing"* is to yoke yourself to Jesus, so His strength is perfected in you. Then, rather than strive with human effort, the Holy Spirit does the work of faith in and through you making you more and more like Jesus. Good works become the overflow of grace in our lives and not an attempt to secure it for ourselves.

We "contend for the faith" when we are mindful not to forget the uncommon cure only Jesus can provide to make our redemption possible.

Resurrected faith rests in "our common salvation," setting contenders' hearts free from dead faith religious works. Our common sickness and side effects have an uncommon cure freely given by grace through faith. The activity of *"faithing"* rests with gratitude for what only Jesus could do, allowing the overflow of grace to produce the good works God intended.

D. – Don't Stop Now

Our journey together in this book nears its end. However, our fight for resurrected faith is far from over because the contenders' purpose is not to learn more head knowledge about Jesus but intimately know Him and the first faith He reveals.

I believe you traveled with me this far because you desire a living faith. Along the way, the Spirit opened our eyes to see how church doctrines were added to or subtracted from the first faith. So, we face the challenge of letting go of some heartfelt beliefs and embracing the truth found in the revelation of Jesus. The heart of a contender has a deep desire to know Jesus. Therefore, we open our hands, allowing the Spirit to restore truths taken away and remove traditions and teaching added to "the faith that was once for all delivered to the saints."

Just as the metamorphosis of "the faith" did not happen overnight, so, too, the renewal of beliefs within the church to align with Jesus' original revelation will not be swift. The work of the Holy Spirit to bring about the needed change of perspective toward various church doctrines takes time.

In the same way, our struggle to contend is not an event with a clear beginning and end. Instead, we have engaged in an ongoing

According to Jesus, when the storms of life come, only those with obedient living faith in His words will be left standing.

process, a pilgrimage that endures for a lifetime. Therefore, we must be vigilant not to think we arrived or can stop in our struggle "to contend for the faith."

When we allow the Holy Spirit to help us begin to struggle for "the faith," Jesus brings us back to life and gives us the heart of a contender. Our dead faith comes alive with resurrection power to transform how we live from the inside out!

Resurrected faith makes us like the wise builder Jesus described at the end of the Sermon on the Mount. The wise hear His words and "does them," building his house upon the rock, while the foolish "does not do them" constructing his home on the sand (Matt. 7:24, 26). When the storms of life come, and sooner or later they hit us all, the wise man's house did not fall because he built it on a firm foundation. But, the dead faith of the foolish man resulted in the total loss of his house because he constructed it on unstable ground.

With the heart of a contender, you joined the struggle for our belief to come alive again. Like a wise builder, dig deep until you hit the bedrock of truth, placing living faith as the cornerstone of your life. Never stop building your life upon this firm foundation with resurrected faith and the activity of *"faithing"* to live what you believe through obedience to Jesus.

Unfortunately, not everyone will contend for "the faith" or choose to look to Jesus and do what He says. However, whatever religious belief one may choose, the importance of their choice to struggle hard for *their faith* cannot be overstated. What an individual believes, and whether or not they take time to think about their beliefs, *their faith* becomes the basis upon which they build their lives.

Faith forms an individual's thinking as their cornerstone regardless of what its kind. These foundational beliefs determine the condition of the groundwork of their lives. But, according to Jesus, when the storms of life come, only those with obedient living faith in His words will be left standing.

People everywhere, of all ages, races, and religious beliefs, are looking for a full, happy life. Jesus promised a better, more fulfilled life than we could ever imagine. We won't find satisfaction in a lifeless religion. People, positions, possessions, or anything else this world may offer also fall short of the fulfillment and happiness we long for in our lives.

Only Jesus promises to give us the abundant life we've always wanted.[10] Resurrected faith to live our beliefs is the key to opening the door to the life we always wanted—a life overflowing with contentment, joy, love, peace, and so much more.

Our continued struggle for a living faith also provides the key to freeing others from the shackles of blinding unbelief and doubt. Our various doctrines present different mental pictures of who Jesus is to people in the world. Only resurrected faith enables us to contend without being contentious, so non-believers see the same love of Jesus living in and through our lives. How you and I fight for the faith will impact whether or not non-believers come to have saving faith in Jesus or not.

Resurrected faith knows Jesus, the cornerstone of our faith, as He is. And by knowing Jesus, you will stand secure in Him upon a firm foundation to enjoy life the way God always intended for it to be.

Your Next Steps

We, Susie and I (Greg), want to help you continue to leave dead faith religion behind. Our prayer is for the LORD to make your faith come alive, no longer sleepwalking through life with dead faith but revived with resurrected faith. So, here's our roadmap with five paths you can take to galvanize your beliefs by daily living in obedience to Jesus' word.

First, continue your *Resurrected Faith* journey with books two and three, *Your Passion to Know Jesus the Cornerstone* and *Winning the Battle for Living Faith.* God gave you the heart of a contender with a growing love for Jesus. Love motivates us in two significant ways. First, deep love continually *learns* and, second, it *protects* one's beloved.

With over forty years of marriage, I appreciate and understand Susie in new and meaningful ways. But, I also stand guard, willing to do anything in my power to protect her because she is my greatest treasure. I'm confident she loves like this too.

The heart of a contender responds the same way towards Jesus. We have a growing passion for knowing and defending Jesus, the one we love.

In *Your Passion to Know Jesus the Cornerstone*, we begin by discovering our blind spots to the good. Dead faith keeps us from seeing Jesus as He is and the work He wants to do in and through our lives. Then with renewed insight, we will focus on Jesus' identity as the eternal God, the prophet like Moses, the coming King of kings, the incarnate God in the flesh, the suffering servant, and the resurrected LORD. Intimate knowledge of Jesus as our cornerstone is essential because our faith is in vain apart from knowing Him.

In *Winning the Battle for Living Faith*, we will see how the contenders' passion motivates us to defend the faith entrusted to us by Jesus. We will, first, allow the Holy Spirit to help us look in the mirror to see the enemy within. Then, we will seek to expose the masquerading wolves who sneak into the church with false teaching to justify their sin. Next, we will look toward the coming judgment day, a warning to keep us from going astray and a plea for the wolves to change their ways before it is too late. Then, we will contrast the dreamer's deadly roads with the narrow lane Jesus calls us to take. Finally, we learn how to contend without being contentious and look again at how to live with resurrected faith, so our beliefs are evident in our words and deeds.

You can continue your journey on a second path to build up your faith with the *Living Faith Journal: Resurrected Faith*. The forty devotions are like a prequel to the book series, showing how many of the ideas shared came from the scriptures and my (Greg's) W.O.R.D. journal. More importantly, you are encouraged to fill this book with your words. You will get more from your Bible reading when you listen to the Holy Spirit speak using the simple acrostic W-O-R-D: Whisper of God, Observation, Real Life Application, and Daily Prayer.

Next, you can dig deeper into God's Word on the third path with the companion study guides for the *Resurrected Faith* book series. Specifically designed to help advance your fight for "the faith," these handbooks will encourage you to apply the message in your daily life, so your faith comes alive. More than questions and answers, we want you to listen to what the LORD says to you and consider how you will respond in obedience to make the needed changes, so with the activity of "faithing," you will live what you believe.

Fourth, while you can complete the study guides on your own, talk with a friend or join a small group at your church to discuss what the LORD is saying to you through *Resurrected Faith*. Whether you go through every question or not, discussing what you wrote in the study guides will help you build accountability through meaningful relationships with other contenders. Remember, with living faith we recognize how much we need each other. Your spiritual growth and maturity develop within a community, but when you remain isolated from other believers, you stifle your growth.

Finally, we invite you to continue your journey by joining us online. We offer a *Resurrected Faith* video course you can complete at your own pace. You are also invited to attend one of our webinars for a conversation with other contenders about how *Resurrected Faith* is helping them to build their lives upon a firm foundation to living what they believe. You can find out more when you visit us online at https://FirmFoundationToday.com/ResFaithOnline. Use the coupon code "R-F-BookSeries" to save 50% on your registration, or email greg@firmfoundationtoday.com to find out about scholarships and additional savings for group registrations.

A Closing Prayer

LORD, thank you for the friends who have joined me here. You have made our faith come alive again, giving us the heart of a contender. Jesus, fan the flame of desire, so our passion never diminishes to know You and "the faith" You reveal. Holy Spirit, continue Your work in us, so the activity of *"faithing"* transforms us from the inside out. Help us be more and more like Jesus to live what we believe, and a world in need of a Savior will come to know You and Your resurrection power.

Contending for Resurrected Faith

✝ Biblical faith is living confidence, trusting God in every area of one's life.

- The activity of *"faithing"* produces a life of surrendered obedience to transform our behavior.

- *"Faithing"* shows the Spirit's activity to write the doctrine of belief upon our hearts, giving us the desire and ability to live what we believe faithfully.

✝ An elementary ABCs framework provides contenders with four necessary reminders to help them persevere in their fight for resurrected faith.

✝ A. – Abide in Christ. Contenders avoid compartmentalizing their lives with a God-awareness of Jesus' daily presence.

- Jesus calls us to all abide in Him because we can do nothing apart from Him.

✝ B. – Be What You Believe. The LORD strengthens contenders to overcome any test, proving our faith is genuine by how we live.

✝ C. – Common Salvation. Contenders understand they can only "contend for the faith" when they embrace the good news gospel and remember our common salvation by:

- Not forgetting the common sickness once infecting our lives held captive with a death sentence in bondage to sin.

o Not ignoring the common side effects of living in a fallen world engaged in a constant tug-of-war between the cravings of our flesh and spirits made alive in Christ.

o Not neglecting the uncommon cure Jesus provides to us through faith and not by works.

✝ D. Don't Stop Now. Contenders realize the fight for "the faith" is an ongoing struggle.

o As wise builders, we dig deep to place faith as the cornerstone of our lives, building upon a firm foundation with obedience to Jesus' words.

o Foolish builders ignore Jesus' words with disobedience, building their lives upon unstable ground.

o Living what we believe determines whether or not we build on a firm foundation to enjoy the abundant, joyful life promised by Jesus.

Notes Chapter 8 "The Heart of a Contender"

[1] Lexicon :: Strong's H87 - **'Aḇrām**. BlueLetterBible.org. Accessed August 5, 2021. https://www.blueletterbible.org/lexicon/h87/esv/wlc/0-1/

[2] Lexicon :: Strong's H85 - **'Aḇrāhām**. BlueLetterBible.org. Accessed August 5, 2021. https://www.blueletterbible.org/lexicon/h85/esv/wlc/0-1/

[3] See: Romans 4:1-8.

[4] See: Romans 6:15-23

[5] See Matthew 4:1-11; Luke 4:1-13.

[6] See Hebrews 2:18.

[7] See Galatians 5:16-26; James 1:13-15.

[8] See Matthew 11:28-30.

[9] See John 10:10.

Don't forget – Sign up for your FREE gift today!
https://firmfoundationtoday.com/free

Tell others what you think of *Resurrected Faith!*

If you enjoyed this book, please consider writing a review at your favorite online bookstore or booklover's site.

Your review and sharing it with your friends is the best gift you could give me as an author. ***Thank you****!*

Acknowledgment

Thank you to Susie, who I affectionately call *"My Bride."* We joined hands in August 1982 and promised to walk side by side through life's journey. Jesus used you to make me into the man I am. You opened my eyes to see how God is at work in me and to find the good in the midst of things I saw as failure. Your encouragement helped me to contend and not give up. Susie, I love you—your confidence in me made the RESURRECTED FAITH series a reality.

I also want to thank my daughter Chrysta Archer for her work to review the initial manuscript. You pushed me for clarity. Your insights challenged me to make the content relevant in today's world. This book would not have become what it is without you.

Heartfelt gratitude to the congregation at Life Church Assembly of God in Garrettsville, Ohio. You loved me and accepted me as your pastor for nineteen years. Special thanks to Bill Butto, Ryan Hartman, Frank Hemphill, Adam Huffman and Noah Siegner, whom God used as "iron sharpens iron" to shape and sharpen my life (Prov. 27:17). You will never know how the LORD used you to teach me how to think deeply and begin to understand what it means to contend for the faith Jesus gave His Church once and for all. As a church you sowed a seed of faith in my heart and released me so the message of resurrected faith could grow and bear fruit in the lives of others.

More Books By the Author

Get the entire *Resurrected Faith Series*

Each of the *Resurrected Faith* books is paired best with its companion Study Guide and your Bible.

Perfect for your Small Group Bible Study.

Visit **www.firmfoundationtoday.com/books**

Look for these titles also!

Change the way you think about money and break free from
the chains of debt that hold you captive with
Finding Financial Freedom.

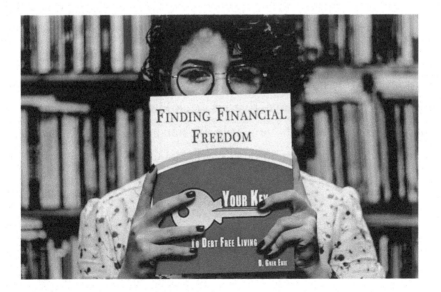

Visit **www.firmfoundationtoday.com/books**

About the Author

D. Greg Ebie is the founder of Firm Foundation with the vision to help people like you have FUEL for Your FIRE—Fuel for Your LIFE. Through his books, live events, and more, Greg helps people live an abundant, happy life by applying the twelve bedrock attitudes to their daily lives.

As an author, Greg is passionate about helping people know Jesus and grow in their faith. He has written eleven books, including the expanded *Resurrected Faith* series with companion study guides. An ordained Assemblies of God minister with over 30 years in full-time pastoral ministry, Greg is now a sought-after speaker and coach.

Greg's bride and best friend Susie have enjoyed life together for over 39 years. They have five adult children who are all happily married. Their favorite new role is Nana and Papa to their six grandchildren. They live in rural Northeast Ohio.

For more information visit
www.firmfoundationtoday.com

Look for
Resurrected Faith
The Heart of a Contender
Now as an Audiobook!

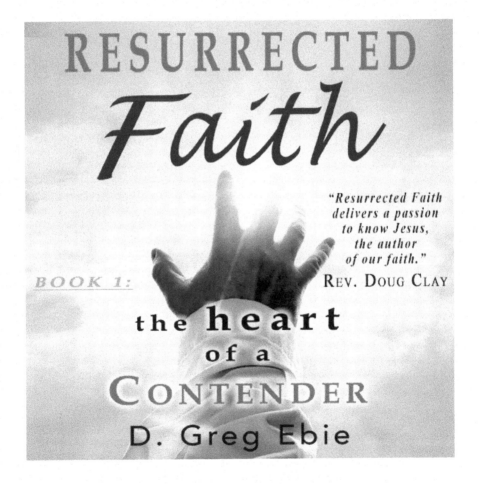

Made in USA - Kendallville, IN
48330_9781736495933
07.19.2022 1336